Cambridge Elements ≡

Elements in Religion and Monotheism
edited by
Paul K. Moser
Loyola University Chicago
Chad Meister
*Affiliate Scholar, Ansari Institute for Global Engagement with Religion,
University of Notre Dame*

T0287021

GOD AND BEING

Nathan Lyons
The University of Notre Dame Australia

CAMBRIDGE
UNIVERSITY PRESS

Shaftesbury Road, Cambridge CB2 8EA, United Kingdom

One Liberty Plaza, 20th Floor, New York, NY 10006, USA

477 Williamstown Road, Port Melbourne, VIC 3207, Australia

314–321, 3rd Floor, Plot 3, Splendor Forum, Jasola District Centre,
New Delhi – 110025, India

103 Penang Road, #05–06/07, Visioncrest Commercial, Singapore 238467

Cambridge University Press is part of Cambridge University Press & Assessment,
a department of the University of Cambridge.

We share the University's mission to contribute to society through the pursuit of
education, learning and research at the highest international levels of excellence.

www.cambridge.org
Information on this title: www.cambridge.org/9781009462518

DOI: 10.1017/9781009026413

© Nathan Lyons 2023

This publication is in copyright. Subject to statutory exception and to the provisions
of relevant collective licensing agreements, no reproduction of any part may take
place without the written permission of Cambridge University Press & Assessment.

First published 2023

A catalogue record for this publication is available from the British Library

ISBN 978-1-009-46251-8 Hardback
ISBN 978-1-009-01276-8 Paperback
ISSN 2631-3014 (online)
ISSN 2631-3006 (print)

Cambridge University Press & Assessment has no responsibility for the persistence
or accuracy of URLs for external or third-party internet websites referred to in this
publication and does not guarantee that any content on such websites is, or will
remain, accurate or appropriate.

God and Being

Elements in Religion and Monotheism

DOI: 10.1017/9781009026413
First published online: December 2023

Nathan Lyons
The University of Notre Dame Australia

Author for correspondence: Nathan Lyons, nathan.lyons@nd.edu.au

Abstract: This Element examines how the Western philosophical-theological tradition between Plato and Aquinas understands the relation between God and being. It gives a historical survey of the two major positions in the period: (a) that the divine first principle is "beyond being" (e.g. Plato, Plotinus, and Pseudo-Dionysius), and (b) that the first principle is "being itself" (e.g. Augustine, Avicenna, and Aquinas). The Element argues that we can recognise in the two traditions, despite their apparent contradiction, complementary approaches to a shared project of inquiry into transcendence.

Keywords: Platonism, theological ontology, being, Plato, Aquinas

ISBNs: 9781009462518 (HB), 9781009012768 (PB), 9781009026413 (OC)
ISSNs: 2631-3014 (online), 2631-3006 (print)

Contents

There is much to say which is hard to perceive about being ... We would have to discover whether God transcends being ... or whether He is Himself being.
                                                            – Origen, *Contra Celsum* VI.64

Introduction

Imagine you have a box containing everything that exists – every rock and tree, every subatomic particle, every person and every galaxy, and every desk chair. If there is more than one universe, all the universes go in the box. If there are immaterial beings such as angels, they go in the box too. Past and future things? In they go. Imagine it is all in your box of being. Now, let us ask a tricky question. Let us assume that the things in the box of being must have been brought into existence by something – we can call this thing the 'origin of being'. Does the origin of being lie *inside* or *outside* your box of existing things?

The question forces us into a dilemma. If we say that the origin of being is outside the box, this means that the cause of existence does not itself exist since we stipulated that all existing things are inside the box of being. But a non-existing cause of existence sounds absurd – it might even sound worse than the problem it is supposed to solve. If we say that the origin of being is inside the box, we have a different challenge. This position gets us an existing first cause, but if the origin is another thing in the box of being, like a chair or a galaxy, then how can it serve as the cause of all these existing things? An in-the-box origin does not solve our problem because we are seeking a causal explanation for all beings in the box, and if the origin is itself one of these beings, then it seems to be just another instance of the question, not a solution to it.

I like to use this thought experiment in my medieval philosophy classes to introduce students to some of the metaphysical puzzles implicit in the idea of transcendence, which is central in so much religious and philosophical thinking in the ancient and medieval period. In particular, this question about the box of being pushes students into one of the perennial difficulties that the Greek philosophical tradition and the Abrahamic religious traditions all grapple with in their own ways: how is the first principle – whether we call it the Good, the One, the First Mover, or God – related to being? This question is the topic of this Element.

We will consider the two leading answers given to this God–being question in Western intellectual traditions during the ancient and medieval periods. The first position is that the first principle is 'beyond being' (BB for short), which is famously articulated by Plato and later Platonists such as Plotinus. The second position is that the first principle is 'being itself' (BI for short), commonly associated with theologians such as Augustine and Thomas Aquinas. In terms of our imagined box of being, BB positions correspond to an origin of being that is 'out of the box'. As we will see, BI positions are more difficult to map on to the thought experiment, with a great deal hanging on the details of how the box of being is characterised.

The scope of this Element is limited to Western traditions of philosophy and theology, though with 'Western' understood expansively to include sources from the Arabic-Islamic world, along with the Greek pagan,[1] Jewish, and Christian traditions. Our period goes roughly from Plato (c. 429–347 BCE) to Thomas Aquinas (1225–1274). I deliberately end our study at this point to dodge Duns Scotus (1265–1308), whose 'univocity of being' doctrine sets a new course for the God–being question and arguably precipitates transformations in subsequent ontological theories that are too complex to address in a study of this size (Boulnois 1999). Our Western focus precludes other traditions that treat comparable themes regarding first principles and being – a larger study might fruitfully compare the Western sources in this study with Hindu Vedanta, Mahāyāna Buddhism, or Confucianism.

In focusing on the core BB and BI positions of premodern Western thought, we will pass over philosophies that propose a first principle that is 'in the box' of being. An obvious instance is the ancient materialists, who posit some physical entity (water, atoms, etc.) as *arche*. Another example is theisms that locate God 'in the box', so that God counts as a 'being among beings'. Such in-the-box theisms were rare in the premodern period – the Stoic god–*logos* is probably an instance,[2] and (as we will see) Aristotle's prime mover is possibly another – but they are more common in later Western intellectual history.

Our inquiry will proceed in four parts:

1. The 'Beyond Being' Tradition
2. The 'Being Itself' Tradition
3. Reconciling the Traditions?
4. God and Being Today

Sections 1 and 2 will offer a loosely chronological, selective survey of BB and BI thinkers in our period. My goal in selecting historical sources has been to illustrate the intellectual development of the traditions over time, with more attention given to more influential sources. Section 3 will consider whether and how the two traditions can be reconciled, given the apparent contradiction between their basic claims. Section 4 will briefly suggest some ways that the findings of our study can inform contemporary philosophy of religion.

---

[1] For want of a better word, I use the term 'pagan' in this study for non-Abrahamic philosophers, acknowledging that the term originates in patristic Christian polemics, not the self-understandings of the philosophers themselves.

[2] See, for example, Alexander of Aphrodisias, *De fato* XXII.

This structure, which divides BB and BI into two separate 'traditions', is inevitably misleading. For better or worse, I place all our historical sources into one or the other tradition, though many sources are ambiguous and reasonable cases could be made for switching some of my decisions. Nevertheless, I think that distinguishing two traditions in this way offers a useful heuristic for interpreting the intellectual history and for clarifying the conceptual issues that are in play. Ultimately, I will argue in Section 3 that BB and BI are complementary ways of articulating transcendence and that there is, in fact, no profound contradiction between the two approaches. The dual structure of this Element will therefore be qualified by the conclusions we draw.

In attempting to cover this wide period of intellectual history, a study of this length will inevitably pass over many complexities in the sources and interpretive debates in current scholarship. This necessity is unfortunate, especially because the God–being question in our period is so complicated and subtle. The sheer variety of 'being' terminologies we will encounter indicates this: Greek (*ousia, ontos,* and *einai*), Hebrew (*hayah*), Arabic (*mawjud, wujud,* and *anniyya*), Latin (*ens, essentia, substantia,* and *esse*), and even a little Coptic (*shoop*) and Middle English (*beyng*). Nevertheless, my hope is that the selective historical surveys presented here will be sufficient to provide an illuminating picture of the development of BB and BI thinking across our period.

One final methodological note before we begin: my working assumption is that, despite their obvious differences, the pagan philosophers and Abrahamic theologians who we consider are pursuing a common intellectual project of conceptualising transcendence, so that the God of the philosophers and the God of Abraham are more or less one and the same, at least according to the self-understandings of the majority of our historical protagonists. I will not try to defend this view historically or conceptually here, though others have.[3] Even with the many disagreements between pagan and Abrahamic traditions and between the Abrahamic traditions themselves, in my view, there is sufficient commonality for them to be meaningfully treated together in a study of this kind.

1 The 'Beyond Being' Tradition

The first of our two God–being traditions claims that the first principle is 'beyond being'. Its leading light is Plato and it is classically expressed in the pagan Neoplatonist tradition, though its influence is present in all the Abrahamic traditions.

---

[3] See, for example, Louth (2007), Marenbon (2006, 1–6), Fraenkel (2015), and Goodman (2012). Compare Hampton and Kenney (2020, 4–5): 'Platonism . . . initiated and sustained a philosophical and theological culture of transcendentalism, centred on the Good or the One. It was this transcendentalism that served as a powerful resource for Jewish, Christian, and Islamic thinkers, generating a distinctive trajectory of thought through its reception into the Abrahamic traditions'.

Plato

The *locus classicus* for BB thinking is Plato's discussion of the Good in *Republic* 509b.[4] In this passage, Socrates is conversing with Glaucon and illustrates his understanding of the Good by a comparison with the sun:

S: You'll be willing to say, I think, that the sun not only provides visible things with the power to be seen but also with coming to be, growth, and nourishment, although it is not itself coming to be.

G: How could it be?

S: Therefore, you should also say that not only do the objects of knowledge owe their being known to the good, but their being is also due to it, although the good is not being [*ouk ousias*], but superior to it [*epekeina tēs ousias*] in rank and power.

And Glaucon comically said: By Apollo, what a daemonic superiority! (509b-c)[5]

As the sun gives light and life to all living things, so Socrates' comparison suggests: the Good gives intelligibility and existence to all beings. As the sun gives growth and change in natural things without itself counting as a changing thing, so the Good gives being to things without itself counting as being or a being – it lies somehow beyond being.

Like all great texts in the history of philosophy – and this is one of the greatest – the interpretation of this passage is highly contested.[6] One possible reading goes like this. In this passage, Socrates serves as a reliable mouthpiece for Plato's own metaphysical views. Here in the *Republic*, Plato construes the world of material things as the realm of becoming (*gignomenou*), which is contrasted with the realm of being (*to on*) (521d), where lie the eternal forms or ideas of material things. This Platonic structure inherits and adapts the foundational Parmenidean-Eleatic notion of being (*on*) as intelligible, change-less, eternal, and one.[7] In the realm of being, there is 'a single form [*idean*] of each' – Plato refers here to the examples of beauty, good, and 'all the things' that are many – and we call this form 'the being [*estin*] of each' (507b). The Good, however, is a special case. It is not just another form, like other forms in the realm of being. The Good is *source* of the truth (*alētheia*) and being (*on*)

---

[4] In addition to the *Republic* and *Parmenides* texts discussed here, other relevant material in Plato includes *Sophist* 242b-251a, *Philebus* 23c-26d, and *Timaeus* 28a-29b.

[5] Trans. (Plato 1992).

[6] For some past and present interpretations, see Baltes (1997), Krämer (2012), and Whittaker (1969).

[7] See Graham (2010, 1:203–44). Indeed, this Parmenidean idea is echoed in one way or another in most historical sources in this study.

enjoyed by all the forms, as the sun is the source of light for physical objects (508d). Therefore, as the source of being, the Good necessarily transcends both the realm of material becoming and the realm of intellectual being – it is not being (*ouk ousias*) but beyond being (*epekeina tēs ousias*). In this passage, Plato gives his account of his first principle: the Good is the extra-ontological first cause, on which all beings depend for their existence.

This brief exposition reflects a traditional interpretation of the *Republic* 509b passage and, while it requires detailed defence against many rival readings today,[8] interpretations along these metaphysical lines were the basis of the text's profound significance in the later BB tradition, especially for the Neoplatonists of the third century onwards.

A second important Platonic source for the BB tradition is the so-called hypotheses of the *Parmenides*. This notoriously difficult dialogue explores puzzles related to the theory of forms and the first principle, described here as 'the One'. In the especially enigmatic second part of the text (137c-166c), the character, Parmenides, probes the ontological status of the One by raising and testing various hypotheses about it. As an initial hypothesis (137c-142a), he considers implications that seem to follow from affirming that 'the one is', that is, affirming that the One exists. These include that the One has no parts, limit, or shape and that it lies outside of time, and so on. These arguments drive to the conclusion that the One in fact *is not*:

> Therefore the one in no way partakes of being [*ousias*] ... the one in no way is [*esti*] ... neither is it in such a way as to be one, because it would then, by being and partaking of being, be [*on kai ousias metechon*]. But, as it seems, the one neither is one nor is [*estin*] ... no name belongs to it, nor is there an account or any knowledge or perception or opinion of it. (141e-142a)[9]

Parmenides' second hypothesis (142b-155e) retraces the same question ('If the one is ... ') but now argues to apparently opposite conclusions. If the One is, then it must be (among other things) whole and infinitely many and have a shape, location, and temporality. The hypothesis concludes that the One must indeed exist in some sense:

> If one is [*estin*], can it be, but not partake of being [*ousias*]? – It cannot. – So there would also be the being of the one, and that is not the same as the one. For if it were, it couldn't be the being of the one, nor could the one partake of it ... Because 'is' signifies something other than 'one' ... So whenever

---

[8] Interpretations akin to this are defended in, for instance, Ferber and Damschen (2015) and Gerson (2020b, 120–93).

[9] Trans. (Plato 1996).

> someone, being brief, says 'one is', [*estin*] would this simply mean that the
> one partakes of being [*ousias*]? (142b-142c)

> Therefore, the one was and is [*estin*] and will be, and was coming to be and
> comes to be and will come to be ... And indeed there would be knowledge
> and opinion and perception of it. (155d)

Again, many interpretations of these difficult passage have been proposed
(Peterson 2019; Turner and Corrigan 2011a, 2011b), and it is certainly beyond
our scope to adjudicate them here. In terms of our box of being, Plato's recondite
arguments here can plausibly be read in support of a principle (or principles) either
in or out of the box, neither, or both. All these possibilities regarding the being/non-
being of the One are investigated in the intricate debate that the *Parmenides*
precipitates in the Platonist tradition – indeed, these *Parmenides* hypotheses are
'so important for subsequent Platonism that this Platonism could not be defined
without it' (Corrigan 2011). A key step in this tradition of debate is an identification
of the two principles described in our texts – the *Republic*'s Good and
Parmenides' – so that the terms can serve as synonymous names for the Platonist
first principle.[10] It is not difficult to see why the two texts are linked by readers in
this way: the being/non-being of the *Parmenides*' One seems to point to the same
peculiar ontological status indicated by the *epekeina* of the *Republic*'s Good.

The Platonists

A first principle 'beyond being' becomes a leading theme in much of the Platonist
tradition after Plato. As we will see, the great exemplar in this respect is Plotinus.
However, before Plotinus, there are some important figures to note. The first is
Plato's nephew and immediate successor as head of the Academy, Speusippus
(408–339 BCE). Aristotle reports that Speusippus believed 'the one itself is not
even an existing thing [*on ti einai*]' (*Meta.* 1092a) and Proclus reports that he
believed 'the One is higher than being and is the source of being' (*In Parm.* VII,
40 K).[11] These and other fragments are complicated to interpret, but they seem
sufficient to locate Speusippus in the BB tradition.[12] After Speusippus, BB thinking
'goes underground' for three centuries,[13] re-emerging in Middle Platonists and

---

[10] Gerson (2020a). There is an old but contested tradition that Plato himself identified the Good and
the One – *agathon estin hen* – in a public lecture titled 'On the Good', which was received with
perplexity or ridicule by its audience (Gaiser 1980). Separate from the more controversial
'unwritten doctrines', there is arguably evidence of the identification in the extant dialogues
(Desjardins 2003, 105–12).

[11] Trans. (Proclus 1992). [12] Dillon (2003, 40–88); Tarán (2016, 86–107).

[13] Carabine (1992b, 45). 'The period of Platonic development from Xenocrates [396–314 BCE]
right down to Antiochus of Ascalon [125–68 BCE], has little to offer to the development of the
idea of the divine transcendent One, apart from the contribution of Speusippus' (37).

Neopythagoreans, beginning in the first-century BCE. Among these, we note Eudorus (first-century BCE), who held that the One is the supreme God (*ton huperanô theon*) and principle (*arche*) of all things, and Moderatus (first-century CE), who holds that 'the first One above Being [*einai*] and all substance ... the second One, which is what really is [*ontos on*] and is intelligible, is the Forms'.[14]

Turning now to Plotinus (204–270), we meet the leading Neoplatonist and probably the leading exponent of 'beyond being' thinking in our period. Plato states only once that the Good is specifically *epekeina ousias* (*Rep.* 509b), but Plotinus takes the remark as the core of his entire metaphysical system. 'While the One is, in truth, ineffable', according to Plotinus, the *Republic* designation is the single appropriate way to speak of it: 'to say "transcends all things and transcends the majesty of Intellect" is, among all other ways of speaking of it, the only true one ... because it indicates that it is not "something" among all things' (V.3.13). He explores the BB status of the first principle – which he variously refers to as the One, the Good, and the God – frequently in his *Enneads*.[15] He emphasises that the One must be construed as beyond being because it transcends the particularity of existing things and ideas, possessing no 'form' that would make it a specific 'this'. The One is not limited to a particular way or kind of being but exceeds the whole array of forms that being may take:

> Since the Substantiality that is generated is form ... the One is necessarily formless. For Substance [*ousian*] must be a 'this something', and this is defined. But it is not possible to grasp the One as a 'this'. For in that case, it would no longer be a principle, but only that thing which you said was a 'this'. But if all things are found within that which is generated, which among these will you say that the One is? Since it is no one of these, it can only be said to transcend them. These are Beings, that is, Being. It, therefore, transcends Being [*epekeina ara ontos*]. (*Enn.* V.5.6)[16]

Because the One is beyond being, it is also beyond intellect, in the senses of both creaturely intelligence and the transcendent hypostasis of Intellect: 'the One is not Intellect, but prior to it. For Intellect is something, whereas the One is not something, because it is prior to every Being, since it is not Being' (*Enn.* VI.9.3). This view is a corollary of Plotinus' conviction, shared with many thinkers in our period, that being and knowledge are coterminous, so that all that exists is knowable, and vice versa.

Plotinus is notable in the BB tradition for making an unambiguous assertion of the first principle's transcendence above being and intellect. As we will see, BB theorists are not always so straightforward. The pagan Neoplatonist

---

[14] Simplicius, *Commentary on Aristotle's Physics*, I.5.181 and I.7.230, trans. (Simplicius 2012).
[15] See esp. *Enn.* V.1, V.4–5, VI.7.   [16] Trans. (Plotinus 2017).

tradition that follows Plotinus often take his unqualified BB position as a litmus test for true Platonism and, therefore, for true philosophy.

Plotinus' student, Porphyry (c. 234–305), speaks in some places in good Plotinian fashion of a principle beyond being. The first principle contains all things 'in the Beyond [*epekeina*], non-intellectually and supra-essentially [*huperousios*]' (*Sent.* 10).[17] The One is 'that which is beyond Intellect [*epekeina tou nou*]' (*Sent.* 25). He even refers to the One as a non-being (*mē on*) beyond being (*huper to on*) (*Sent.* 26). These BB-style remarks, however, must be set alongside hostile reports from later Neoplatonists that Porphyry, abandoning authentic Plotinianism, identified his first principle as 'the summit of the intelligible world' (Proclus, *In Parm.* 1070) or 'the Father of the intelligible triad' (Damascius, *De prin.* VII.43).[18] These reports allege that Porphyry's first principle is, in fact, Being, which is the first of three elements in the Neoplatonist 'intelligible realm' (i.e. the Being–Life–Intellect triad). This apparently non-Plotinian, BI-style view of Porphyry is significantly strengthened if one accepts, as some do, the Porphyrian authorship of the *Anonymous Commentary on Plato's Parmenides*, which we will discuss in our BI survey. Considering only his generally accepted texts, Porphyry is ambiguous.

Later Neoplatonists endorse Plotinus' BB position. Iamblichus (c. 242–325) contrasts 'the good that is beyond being [*epekeina tēs ousias*]' with 'that which exists on the level of being' (*De mysteriis* I.5).[19] Proclus (412–485) agrees that 'the good is, as we say, beyond being and is the source of beings' and argues that 'the good is better than absolute being' (*De malo.* 2).[20] Damascius (c. 480–550) observes that because 'it is altogether impossible to conceive of anything simpler than the One', we must conclude that 'in every way ... the One is before Being' (*De prin.* II.21).

However, later Neoplatonists also complicate the Plotinian account of the One, in an effort to explain more convincingly how the single principle is related to the multiplicity of beings that flow from it, they present various depictions of a 'realm of the One' emerge,[21] often populated by multiple principles beyond being. Iamblichus proposes a hierarchy of (a) the Ineffable (*pantelōs arrheton*), (b) the transcendent One-beyond-the-One, (c) the One, which is 'one simply' (*ho haplos hen*) and contains all beings 'in a hidden mode', and (d) the principles of Limited and the Unlimited, with the whole structure located beyond being.[22] Damascius similarly contrasts the highest Ineffable, to which no attributes can be affirmed or

---

[17] Trans. (Porphyry 2005).   [18] Trans. (Damascius 2009).   [19] Trans. (Iamblichus 2003).
[20] Trans. (Proclus 2014).
[21] This is Sara Ahbel-Rappe's useful analytical term in Damascius (2009).
[22] As reported in Damascius *De prin.* VII.43, VIII.50–51, and Proclus *In Parm.* 1066 and *In Tim.* I.78. In Iamblichus' system, the highest principle within being is a third One – the One-Existent (*to hen on*).

denied, with a One, which 'is the principle of all things' and is identified with the principle Plato describes as the Good or One beyond being (*De prin.* I.1–8; II.22). Syrianus (d. 437), the teacher of Proclus, similarly proposed that 'beyond the One there will be a unique principle, the Ineffable' (Damascius, *De prin.* IV.10). A key issue in these intra-Neoplatonist debates is the interpretation of *Parmenides* hypotheses discussed earlier.

Yet, more complexity emerges in the realm of the One with the doctrine of *henads*. Beneath or around the *hen* (the One), we find *henads* (unities), which Proclus also describes as 'gods' (*theoi*).[23] The *henads* are like the One in every way except that they are 'participated' – that is, lower beings can share in their qualities – while the One is strictly unparticipated (*El. Th.* prop. 116).[24] However, like the One, the *henads* are beyond being: 'if the First Principle transcend Being, then since every god [i.e. every *henad*], qua god, is of the order of that Principle, it follows that all of them must transcend Being [*huperousios*]' (*El. Th.* prop. 115).

There are occasionally instances of Latin BB thinking outside or adjacent to the mainstream Latin Christian tradition (Gersh 1986, 419–646). One is Calcidius (fourth century), who describes his first principle as 'the highest God, who is the supreme Good, beyond all substance [*ultra omnem substantiam*] and all nature' (*In Tim.* 176),[25] likely echoing the *Republic* text.[26]

From Good to God

Before moving to the Abrahamic traditions, we must note how the talk about the Good and One in pagan Platonists is related to theological talk about God/s. Theological (*theos*) language is present in virtually all Greek discussions of first principles, from the Presocratics forward (Drozdek 2016). Theological talk is everywhere in the Platonist tradition. Xenocrates (339–314 BCE) in the Old Academy describes the One as 'first God' (fr. 213).[27] All Middle Platonists see their primary principle as a god, and most see it as a divine intellect in which the Platonic forms are contained or produced (Boys-Stones 2017, 147–83). Plotinus describes the One in theological terms with some frequency (Rist 1962). The theological dimension is especially obvious in the later Neoplatonists. Proclus argues that 'God and One are the same because there is nothing greater than God and nothing greater than the One' (*In Parm.* I.641). In a particularly illuminating

---

[23] See, for exampe, Proclus, *El. Th.* props. 113–27. The term *henads* has an earlier history – for example, Plato, *Philebus* 15a; Plotinus, *Enn.* VI.6.
[24] Trans. (Proclus 1963).   [25] Trans. (Calcidius 2016).
[26] Though there are ambiguities regarding the ontological status of Calcidius' first God – see Reydams-Schils (2020, 88–96).
[27] See Gerson (2008, 96–7).

sentence, he identifies One, Good, and God beyond being: 'that the One [*hen*] is God [*theos*] follows from its identity with the Good [*agathon*]: for the Good is identical with God, God being that which is beyond [*epekeina*] all things' (*El. Th.* prop. 113). Additionally, the Neoplatonist tradition increasingly pursues religious and liturgical practices, particularly the ritual theurgy recommended by Iamblichus and Proclus (Addey 2016).

The free movement between philosophical and theological vocabularies (if it makes sense to distinguish these at all) in Platonist metaphysical speculation supports the view that pagan and Abrahamic thinkers in our period are engaged in a common intellectual inquiry into transcendence. It is no great novelty for the Abrahamic theologians to identify the one Good with the one God because the basic link is already present in the Platonist tradition.

The Abrahamic Traditions

Eastern Christians

The Platonist 'beyond being' tradition is embraced by many theologians in the Greek Eastern Christian tradition. The formative figure is Pseudo-Dionysius the Areopagite (c. fifth–sixth century). Under the influence especially of Proclus, Dionysius constantly refers to the Christian God as 'beyond being'. The task of theology is to deal 'with what is beyond being [*huperousiois*]' (*Div. nom.* 641D).[28] God is 'the supra-being beyond every being [*huperousios apases ousias*]' (648C). The Trinity is the 'divine unity beyond being', enjoying a 'supra-essential subsistence [*huperousios huparxis*]' (641A). God's transcendence of being goes together with a strict apophatic transcendence of language and knowledge:

> [He] transcends [*huper*] mind and being [*ousian*]. He is completely unknown and non-existent [*mēde einai*]. He exists beyond being [*estin huperousios*] and he is known beyond [*huper*] the mind. (*Epist.* 1)[29]

> [T]he unknowing of what is beyond being [*huperousiotetos*] is something above and beyond speech, mind, or being itself ... [B]eings are surpassed by the infinity beyond being [*huperousios apeiria*], intelligences by that oneness which is beyond intelligence. (*Div. nom.* 588A-B)

These BB commitments are confirmed in Dionysius' recognition of *Good* as the highest divine name, in keeping with the Platonists: 'the sacred writers have pre-eminently set apart [*Good*] for the supra-divine God from all other names' (693B).

---

[28] Trans. (Pseudo-Dionysius 1987).   [29] Trans. (Pseudo-Dionysius 1987).

Yet, alongside these many BB descriptions of God as an extra-ontological principle, Dionysius expounds with approbation the divine name of 'Being', which appears second only to 'Good' (816A-825C). Alluding to Exodus 3:14, he instructs his readers to celebrate 'the name of "being" which is rightly applied by theology to him who truly is' (816B). Further, he argues that God possesses 'preexistence' (*proeinai*) (820B) and that God has an 'existence' above being (*huperousios einai*) (824A). The Good 'is' beyond being (*to ontos huperousio*) (687A) and God 'is the essence of being [*to einai*] for the things which have being [*onta*]' (817D).

Yet again, however, all of this is apparently exceeded by his view that God transcends being *and* non-being. Dionysius appears in places to identify God with non-being, for example, 'nothing is completely a non-being [*mē on*], unless it is said to be in the Good in the sense of beyond-being [*huperouison*]' (716D). Elsewhere, he elevates God above the non-being/being contrast: God is 'absolute goodness, surpassing the things that are and the things that are not' (736B). The name *Good* 'extends to beings and non-beings and that Cause is superior [*huper*] to being and nonbeings' (816B). The implication seems to be that the transcendence of the Good is so great as to include the plenitude of being itself, yet also to exceed it and capture too the non-existent and not-yet-existent.

What should we make of this 'untidiness ... or, perhaps, paradox' (Louth 2001, 87) in Dionysius regarding BB and BI? In my view, he is best read as finally a BB thinker. As several scholars emphasise, Dionysius' Neoplatonist view of being as intelligible and finite means that Dionysius' infinite God must finally exceed being and his positive ascriptions of being should be seen as recognitions that God pre-contains being as its cause (O'Rourke 1992, 65–84; Perl 2007, 5–34).[30]

In part because of his assumed status as an apostolic figure, Dionysius is enormously influential in both Eastern and Western Christian traditions – as Palamas remarks, Dionysius is 'the most prominent of theologians next to the divine apostles' (*Capita* 85)[31] – and all major Eastern theologians respond in some way to Dionysius' doctrine of God beyond being. Maximus the Confessor (c. 580–662) is a good example. 'God', writes Maximus, 'is simply and indefinably beyond all beings [*huper panta ta onta*] ... beyond reason and knowledge and any kind of relationship whatever' (*Ambigua* 10, 1153B).[32] He

---

[30] O'Rourke (1992, 202): 'expressing the ontological transcendence of the Thearchy with such phrases as *ontos proon* or *on estin huperousios*, Dionysius is relying upon entitative words and concepts to express the immeasurable distance between the finite and infinite ... *ontos* is used to convey the supra-existential excellence of the Good but is itself proper to existence, which, according to Dionysius, is necessarily finite'. We will return to the theme of infinite being in the following.

[31] Trans. (Palamas 1988).   [32] Trans. (Louth 1996).

explains: 'being [*einai*] is derived from [God], but he is not being [*einai*]. For he is beyond being itself [*einai*]' (1180D). Yet, like Dionysius, Maximus still speaks in ontological terms about God, variously attributing 'being itself' (*auto to einai, autoousia*) and 'beingness' (*ontotes*) to God (Perl 1991, 114). He argues that 'God always properly is, one and alone by nature, comprehending in himself all proper being [*kurios einai*] in every way, as being above proper being itself' (*Capita theo. eco.* 1084C).[33] In an important and delicate passage, Maximus explains that God's peculiar ontological status means that being and non-being are both fittingly applied, though under apophatic constraints:

> [God] can in no way be associated by nature with any being and thus because of his superbeing [*huperontos*] is more fittingly referred to as nonbeing … In fact both names, being [*to einai*] and nonbeing [*to mē einai*], are to be reverently applied to him although not at all properly. In one sense they are both proper to him, one affirming the being of God as cause of beings, the other completely denying in him the being which all beings have, based on his preeminence as cause. On the other hand, neither is proper to him because neither represents in any way an affirmation of the essence of the being under discussion as to its substance or nature … He has in fact a simple existence [*huparxin*], unknowable and inaccessible to all and altogether beyond understanding which transcends all affirmation and negation. (*Mystagogia* proem 664AC)[34]

John Damascene (c. 676–749), apparently departing from Dionysius, gives pride of place to 'being' as a divine name: 'of all the names given to God the more proper is that of He Who Is [*ho on*] … for like some limitless and boundless sea of essence [*ousias apeiron*], He contains all being in Himself' (*De fide* I.9).[35] However, this sits alongside Dionysian BB claims – indeed, he immediately follows this sentence with: 'but as St. Dionysius says, He is The Good, for in God one may not say that the being comes first and then the good afterwards'. God, he explains, 'transcends [*huper*] all beings [*onta*] and being itself [*autode to einai on*]' (*De fide* I.4). He is 'superessential [*huperousion*] and unnameable'; so the most satisfactory way to refer to his being is 'superessential essence [*huperousion ousia*]' (*De fide* I.12).

In the fourteenth century, Gregory Palamas (c. 1296–1357) expressed similar BB convictions. God 'is not a being [*on estin*] … he is not being [*on*] because he is beyond all beings [*huper panta ta onta*]' (*Capita* 78). And elsewhere: 'we say that that God is not being, for we believe Him to be above being' (*Triads* II.iii.8).[36] While Palamas does use the language of *ousia* in theological argument, he clarifies

---

[33] Trans. (Perl 1991, 114).   [34] Trans. (Berthold 1985).   [35] Trans. (Damascene 1958).
[36] Trans. (Palamas 1983).

that, properly speaking, God is 'superessential' (*huperousios*), an 'essence beyond essence' (*ousia huperousios*).[37] He explains that 'the superessential … is the reality which possesses [divine] powers and gathers them into unity in itself' (*Triads* III.i.23). He thus locates God as beyond beings 'in a superessential [*huperousios*] way' (*Triads* I.iii.8) and argues, stretching his Dionysian terminology, that God 'possesses the superessential superessentially' (*Triads* III.iii.14).

Western Christians

BB positions are rare in the Western Latin tradition. John Scottus Eriugena (815–877), however, is an outstanding counterexample. With facility in Greek, he engages closely with Maximus and Dionysius, whom he sees as 'the highest theologian' (*Periphyseon* III 644b),[38] and develops a remarkable Latin rendition of BB in the wake of these Eastern theologians. 'The ineffable Nature', he writes, 'is not called Essence properly, yet it is properly called superessential [*superessentialis*]' (I 460c). God is 'the Goodness beyond being [*superessentialis bonitas*]' (III 619c), and he 'alone properly subsists above being itself [*super ipsum esse*]' (I 481c). Like many BB theologians, Eriugena still uses BI language. The origin of things 'is Being itself [*ipsum esse*], which indeed is God, Who gives both being [*esse*] (as a natural gift) and wellbeing (as a grace)' (I 515b). And 'when we say that God *is* [*esse*], we do not say that He is after some manner … we use the words *is* [*est*] and *was* [*erat*] in Him simply and infinitely and absolutely' (I 482a). Nevertheless, these attributions of divine being must be interpreted in light of, and probably subordinated to, Eriugena's attributions of 'non-being' or 'nothingness' to God, which he argues indicate excellence, not privation:

> [S]o long as it is understood to be incomprehensible by reason of its transcendence it is not unreasonably called 'Nothing' [*nihilum*] … the Divine Goodness [is] called 'Nothing' for the reason that, beyond all things that are and that are not, it is found in no essence (III 680d-681c)

or:

> [W]hen we predicate being of Him we do not say that He is [*non dicimus ipsum esse*]; for being is from Him but He is not Himself being [*non ipsum esse*]. For above this being after some manner there is More-than-being [*superesse*]. (I 482b)

Indeed, some interpreters suggest that, on balance, Eriugena's theological ontology is better described as a 'negative ontology' or meontology, which

---

[37] Pino (2022, 50–5).   [38] Trans. (Sheldon-Williams 1968).

'can be read as an alternative to a metaphysics based on Exodus 3:14' (Carabine 2000, 41; Moran 2004, 92–102). The Latin tradition will not see anything quite like this bold expression of BB thinking again until Meister Eckhart in the thirteenth century.

Jews and Muslims

As in the Latin Christian tradition, the majority of the Jewish and Islamic medieval thinkers fall on the side of BI. In the Jewish tradition, BB thinking is relatively rare.[39] One instance may be the medieval Kabbalists, who describe the divine principle as *Ein-Sof* (infinite) and occasionally attribute to it *yitron* (superfluity), a term which Gershom Scholem suggests in his classic study is 'apparently as a translation of the neoplatonic term *hyperousia*' (Scholem 1974, 89). If we are willing to count them in the Jewish tradition, an earlier instance may be the Sethian Gnostics (second–third century). One typical Sethian text says of 'the pure One' that it 'is not anything among existing things, but rather something superior to these – not "superior" in the comparative sense, but in the absolute sense'.[40]

In the Islamic-Arabic tradition, there are some Neoplatonist-influenced streams that hold explicitly to a BB position (Kars 2019; Morewedge 1992). An early instance is Jahm bin Safwan (696–745), who argued that God is not 'a being [*say*'] since a being is something created' and 'this would be to make Him similar to beings [*'asya*']'. While God is 'not a being ... neither is He a non-being [*la say*'] because He is the Creator of all *beings* so there is no *being* which is not a creature'.[41]

A more sustained Islamic BB stream is the tenth–eleventh century tradition of Neoplatonic Isma'ili thinkers. Al-Sijistani (c. 930–971) is a leading figure, who writes: 'the word Allah has two syllables and likewise exaltation is of two kinds: exaltation above beingness [*al-aysiya*] and exaltation above nonbeingness [*al-laysiya*]' (*Kitab al Yanabi* sec. 111).[42] Even the transcendent principle of intellect, the 'Preceder', defers to Allah's extra-ontological transcendence: the Preceder 'sees that the greatness of its Originator is something it does not have the ability to grasp and thus it must exalt Him above every being and nonbeing' (sec. 110). Similarly, Nasir Khusrav (1004–1088) argues that, while the Intellect

---

[39] Sarah Pessin (2003) makes a compelling case for continuities between Plotinus' and Ibn Gabirol's first principle, but I think Gabirol is still better situated in the BI tradition, as I will argue in the next section).

[40] *Apocryphon of John*, Berlin Codex 24–5, trans. (Turner 2001, 503). The Sethian Gnostic texts are complex to interpret and I discuss them again in the BI tradition in the following.

[41] These quotations are from later reports in Ibn Hanbal and others, all translated in Frank (2005).

[42] Trans. (Al-Sijistānī 1994).

(*Aql*) is 'the First Existent', God himself 'is beyond being or not-being' (*Shish Fasl* chap. 1 and 2).[43] This Isma'ili BB view was fiercely opposed by some later Sunnis and – in an episode that reveals how perilously high the stakes can climb in BB–BI debates – the young mystic philosopher Ayn al-Quzat Hamadani (1098–1131) was executed by Seljuk rulers,[44] who claimed to hear heretical echoes of Isma'ili ideas in his claim that God is 'source' (*masdar*) of existence: 'it is God who is the source [*masdar*] of existence in all the diversity of its genera and species' (*Zubdat al-ḥaqa'iq* chap. 4).[45]

The Logic of BB

Reflecting on this survey of the premodern BB tradition, we can identify a few core convictions and arguments that commonly underlie BB thinking in our period.

Beyond Knowledge and Language

For BB thinkers, the first principle exceeds our capacity to intellectually comprehend or linguistically express its nature. All BB thinkers hold to some version of this apophaticism. (As we will see, it is a commonplace too in the BI tradition.) Plato, for instance, says of the One that 'no name belongs to it, nor is there an account or any knowledge or perception or opinion of it' (*Parmenides* 141e).[46] Plotinus says that 'nothing can be predicated of' the One and so 'we say what it is not; what it is, we do not say' (*Enn.* III.8.10, V.3.14). The first principle 'is altogether outside the realm of language, and it is not knowable in any way at all', argues Damascius, and it can only be revealed by 'the complete overturning of discourse and thought' (*De prin.* I.7). 'As we plunge into that darkness which is beyond intellect', Dionysius warns, 'we shall find ourselves not simply running short of words but actually speechless and unknowing' (*Myst. theo.* 1033B-C).[47] A conviction often in the background of these apophatic approaches is the identity of being and thinking, which was first articulated by Parmenides and echoes through Greek philosophy and the Abrahamic traditions.[48] As the first principle exceeds being, so it exceeds thought and language, which articulates our thought. John Damascene states this nexus of ideas succinctly: 'As regards what God is, it is impossible to say what He is in His essence ... [for] He transcends all beings and being itself. And, if

---

[43] Trans. (Khusrav 1949).
[44] Political antagonisms are also important in this incident (Safi 2006, 158–200).
[45] Trans. (al-Quḍāt 2022). Compare. xvii.   [46] Trans. (Plato 1996).
[47] Trans. (Pseudo-Dionysius 1987).
[48] See Perl (2014). Parmenides: 'the same is for thinking and for being' (frag. 3).

knowledge respects beings, then that which transcends knowledge will certainly transcend essence, and, conversely, what transcends essence will transcend knowledge' (*De fide* I.4).

Not a Being among Beings

'Is the so-called one principle of all things beyond all things', asks Damascius, 'or is it one among all things, as if it were the summit of those that proceed from it?' (*De prin.* I.1). All BB thinkers know the answer to this question. It refers to the most basic conviction of BB theory: the first principle cannot be 'a being' among beings or 'a thing' among things. It cannot even be the 'highest being' among beings; it must lie beyond beings and being entirely. If the first principle is to be truly first, it must be the cause of the existence of things, and it therefore cannot be one of those things whose existence one is seeking to explain – returning to our box metaphor, if the First is in the box of being, then it is just another instance of the origin-of-being question, not an answer to it. As Proclus succinctly puts it, 'inasmuch as it is the cause of all things, it is no one of all things' (*In Parm.* VI.1108). Or yet more succinctly, Plotinus: 'The cause of everything is none of these things' (*Enn.* VI.9.6).

Therefore, BB thinkers are constantly denying any entitative status to the first principle, as we saw repeatedly in our survey of sources – 'he is not a being [*on estin*] ... because he is beyond all beings [*huper panta ta onta*]' (Palamas, *Capita* 78). Further, BB thinkers frequently deny that the first principle is in any sense a 'what' or a 'this' and set it apart from the formal determinacy that is characteristic of beings. Thus, according to Plotinus: 'substance must be a "this something" ... [but] "that which transcends Being" does not indicate a "this" ... but implies only that it is not this' (*Enn.* V.5.6). For these reasons, the BB tradition often strikes a meontological note, as we saw especially with Dionysius and Eriugena.

Immanence

However, this BB emphasis on extra-ontological transcendence should not be understood deistically as indicating a God distant or absent from beings. Indeed, BB thinkers tend to see the transcendence of the One as the very reason why it is so immanent to beings. Plotinus argues that because the One is not located and therefore restricted to a particular place, it is therefore present to everywhere and everything: 'as for things which are not somewhere, there is nowhere they are not' (*Enn.* V.5.9). Dionysius argues that God, 'is the being immanent in and underlying the things which are' and this is possible because 'He is not [*oute estin*]. Rather he is the essence of being for the things which have being' (*Div.*

nom. 817D). While the addition of extra principles beyond being in later Neoplatonists can look like a worried attempt to further distance the first principle from the world by adding yet more intermediaries – the 'bureaucratic fallacy'[49] – this can be read, on the contrary, as an attempt to more emphatically affirm immanence since the Ineffable is, according to Damascius, 'over the one and the many' (*De prin.* I.1.8) and, therefore, is as 'close' to the multiplicity of beings as it is to transcendent unity.[50]

Being Is Finite

In the BB tradition, being is typically assumed to be finite, not infinite.[51] There is occasional positive appreciation of the infinite in Greek philosophical tradition before Plotinus, for example, Anaximander's *apeiron arche*, some atomists' infinite void and infinite atoms. But the majority view among the Greeks is that infinity implies indefiniteness and indeterminacy, while *being* means to be a definite and finite thing; a definable and knowable entity determined by a particular form. Infinity thus tends to comport imperfection. 'Nothing is complete which has no end and the end is a limit', Aristotle argues, and so the infinite is contrasted with the 'complete and whole' and 'its essence is privation' (*Physics* 207a, 207b).[52] The Aristotelian-Platonist traditions tend to link being with form, order, determinacy, and completion, and, in this context, 'infinite being' is a contradiction in terms. Plotinus complicates this picture by construing the One's indeterminacy as a perfection: 'it is something other than all the things to which "what it is" applies ... it is indefinite [*aoristos*]' (*Enn.* VI.8.9); it is 'unlimited [*apeiros*] ... by being incomprehensible in its power' (VI.9.6). However, for Plotinus, this infinity is precisely what distinguishes the One from being,[53] which remains finite.

It seems that the possibility of infinite being properly speaking emerges, as we will see in our BI survey, only with the Anonymous Commentator's and Victorinus' indeterminate and infinitival *to einai/esse* and Gregory of Nyssa's infinite divine substance.

---

[49] See, for example, Osborn (1993, 15).   [50] Cf. Milbank (2010) and Shaw (1995).

[51] Sweeney (1992); Undusk (2009). With some qualifications, Undusk (2009, 308) observes: 'not before Christianity and Neoplatonism (Plotinus), was infinity assigned in the Greek mind a significant cognitive value, let alone elevating it to the position of highest perfection'.

[52] Trans. (Aristotle 1984b).

[53] John Rist (1967, 25) argues that, in Plotinus: 'in view of the general Greek use of "Being" to mean "finite Being," the prima facie meaning of the phrase "beyond Being" should be "infinite Being"'. However, some critics charge that this misunderstands Plotinus: 'not because of an accidental restriction on the usage of the term "being," but because of the philosophically grounded principle that to be is to be intelligible, being necessarily entails finitude' (Perl 2007, 12); see also Sweeney (1992, 239–41).

It is not difficult to see how this conviction about the finitude of being factors into BB deliberations about the first principle. If the first principle is to be properly transcendent, then it must be beyond being, because being is particular, formed, and finite, and these characteristics unduly restrict the First's unlimited transcendence.

Is BB a Species of Atheism?

Lastly, we must comment on a strangeness in BB thinking that we first noted in our box of being thought experiment. If God is beyond existence, then this seems to entail that God does not exist. But doesn't this mean that all BB thinkers must be atheists?

This question recalls Jean-Luc Marion's lament that his book, *God Without Being*, 'suffered from the inevitable and assumed equivocation of its title: was it insinuating that the God "without being" is not, or does not exist?' (1995, xix). Marion replies: 'Let me repeat now the answer I gave then: no, definitely not. God is, exists, and that is the least of things'. Marion's remark can, I think, answer for the BB tradition too. There is a common-sense way in which all BB thinkers are 'theists' (or, if you like, 'henologists'), in the sense that a transcendent first principle is *there* at the head of their metaphysical systems. Denying the principle's existence in this common-sense meaning would be tantamount to saying that BB thinkers are aligned with philosophers who posit no transcendent, unitary *arche* in their systems, such as the ancient atomists. This is obviously false. Taken in a common-sense way, BB thinkers affirm the existence of the Good, the One, and the God. To adapt a Derridean phrase, they rightly pass for theists.

But as Marion says – with a hint of impatience – this fact 'is the least of things'. Recognising *that* there is a transcendent first principle is only the beginning of BB inquiry. What is of deeper philosophical interest is the nature of this principle and its curious extra-ontological standing in relation to beings. We therefore should not let the common-sense affirmation of theism domesticate the BB language of *epekeina*, but, instead, let it do the difficult-to-understand, metaphysically revisionary work that BB thinkers intend it to do. For BB thinkers, the first principle is indeed extra-ontological and it should not be construed as in any sense 'a being' that 'exists' in the way beings exist, even if our grammar requires us to sometimes speak in this way to carry on the philosophical conversation. The meontological streak in the BB tradition especially indicates this. If we worry that these BB claims diminish the first principle – 'the One, like an illusion, doesn't even exist' – then we have missed the BB point. The point of this language is not that God is 'less' than being but that he is somehow 'more' than being. Thus, according to John Damascene: 'for

He does not belong to the number of beings [*onton*], not because He does not exist [*mē on*], but because He transcends all beings and being itself' (*De fide* I.4).

Depending on one's philosophical inclinations, the paradoxical language that is sometimes present in this BB talk about the first principle may seem either a great virtue or a great vice of the tradition. But from a BB point of view at least, such talk is a principled attempt to articulate the logic of transcendence, which requires a first principle that is 'outside the box' of being.

2 The 'Being Itself' Tradition

Our second God–being tradition holds that the first principle should be identified with being – it is 'being itself'. Variations of this BI view become dominant in the Abrahamic traditions through the Middle Ages, but, like the BB tradition, its roots extend back to Greeks.

The Greeks

We began the BB tradition with Plato, and we begin our survey of the BI tradition with Plato's student, Aristotle (384–322 BCE). The change and coming-to-be that is ubiquitous in nature occurs, according to Aristotle, through the actualising of latent potentialities in things – for example, a tree emerges by the actualising of biological potencies in a seed. Aristotle argues that these processes require an ultimate explanation, which can only be supplied by an originary cause that is fully actual and without any potency. This cause is the First Mover: 'one actuality always precedes another in time right back to the actuality of the eternal prime mover' (*Meta.* 1050b).[54] It is 'a mover which moves without being moved, being eternal, substance [*ousia*], and actuality [*energeia*]' (*Meta.* 1072a). In ascribing being (*ousia*) to his First Mover, Aristotle departs from the Platonist thought of a first principle *epekeina tēs ousias*, beyond being.[55] He also establishes the first principle's unique status in a different way – where the Platonists emphasise a peculiar relation to *ousia* as the defining trait of the Good/One, Aristotle uses his actuality–potency framework to emphasise the peculiarly 'actual' character of his first substance. Further, he describes the First Mover in explicitly intellectual and theological terms: 'the actuality of thought is life, and God is that actuality [*energeia*]'

---

[54] Trans. (Aristotle 1984a).

[55] On the other hand, in a fragment of *On Prayer* reported by Simplicius, Aristotle alludes sympathetically to the idea of a God *epekeina* mind, and implicitly *epekeina* being – but even here he still seems to put aside the view of his teacher: 'Aristotle reduces the Good-itself to *nous*, dispensing with the mysterious Good which Plato had posited, beyond *nous* and *ousia*' (Menn 1992). Cf. Plotinus' implicit critique of Aristotle's first mover in *Enn.* V.6.

(*Meta.* 1072a). Thus, Aristotle's first principle is a God who is intellect (*nous*), substance (*ousia*), and act (*energeia*). Each of these characteristics will be important in the subsequent BI tradition.

The next major Greek contributors to BI theory are the Middle Platonists.[56] Plutarch (c. 45–120) says that god 'is one, and fills eternity in a single moment; he alone really exists [*ontos on*] and does not change' (*On the E at Delphi*, 393B). Alcinous (second century) writes that 'the first god is eternal, ineffable ... complete in every respect: he is divinity, being [*ousiotes*], truth, symmetry, good' (*Didaskalikos* 10). Numenius (second century) is an especially interesting case. He describes his first God as 'the first intellect, which is called "being itself" [*autoon*]' (fr. 17) and he describes his first God as *ho on* (fr. 13). Yet, there are BB echoes in Numenius, as when he describes the Good as 'principle of substance [*agathon ousias einai archē*]' (fr. 16). This BB–BI ambiguity may be deliberate. In an unforgettable image, Numenius compares the Good to a little fishing boat, glimpsed bobbing between waves:

> Imagine someone sitting at the top of a lookout: he catches a quick glimpse of a small fishing boat – one of those solitary light skiffs, alone, in solitude, caught between waves – and he recognises it. So must one retreat far from the objects of perception to join alone with the Good which is alone ... [in] an ineffable, a completely indescribable, divine solitude. There are the haunts of the Good, its pastimes and festivals; but it, in peace, in benevolence, the calm, the gracious ruler, rides upon being [*ousia*]. (fr. 2)

This picture of the Good floating on a surface, sailing upon being, seems deliberately calibrated to position the Good as simultaneously above and within being (Dillon 2007).

In the background of Middle Platonist views are differing strategies for synthesising various Platonic texts. Many attribute being positively to the Good, sometimes in an attempt to conform the *Republic* 509b's *epekeina* with other apparently ontological descriptions in the *Republic* – for example, the Good is the 'brightest part of being [*ontos*]' (518c), the 'happiest of being [*ontos*]' (526e), and the 'best among beings [*ousi*]' (532c) (Baltes 1997; Whittaker 1969).[57] Different thinkers attempt to either identify or distinguish the *Republic*'s Good and the *Timaeus*' demiurge, whose intellectual and creative activity seems to demand a position within being (Kenney 2010, 57–90; O'Brien 2015). And some attempt to integrate all this with the hypotheses of

---

[56] Unless otherwise noted, Middle Platonist quotations in this section are from Boys-Stones (2017).

[57] Matthias Baltes (1997, 22): 'all Platonists before Plotinus confirm ... that Plato's Idea of the Good is not *epekeina tou ontos*. For according to all these interpreters of Plato's philosophy, the Idea of the Good is something like the highest being, *to on auto*, which bestows upon all other things their being'.

the *Parmenides* (Turner and Corrigan 2011a). These developments in the Middle Platonist period propel a general move toward BI versions of Platonism, though often with residual ambiguities. As Whittaker sums up: 'there existed in the minds of writers of the Middle Platonic period a confusion concerning the status of the ultimate principle with reference to *ousia* and *nous*' (1969, 104).

The God of Exodus

We turn now to BI themes in the Abrahamic traditions. On this score, there is one intellectual-historical moment that must be noted above all: the Greek Septuagint translation of Exodus 3:14 (c. third–second century BCE). In this biblical passage, God declares his name to Moses:

> God said to Moses, 'I AM WHO I AM' [*Ehyeh asher Ehyeh / ego eimi ho on*].
> He said further, 'Thus you shall say to the Israelites, "I AM [*Ehyeh / ho on*] has sent me to you"'.[58]

The Septuagint rendering of the Hebrew as *ego eimi ho on* becomes a common form in which the text is received by philosophers and theologians in the Hellenistic and Roman periods (Wilkinson 2015, 44–122). Whereas contemporary translators tend to render the Hebrew original into English as something like 'I will be what I will be', the Septuagint phrase conveys something like 'I am the Self-Existent'. Metaphysical interpretations of the language flourished, and the seminal figure in this interpretive tradition is the Hellenistic Jewish philosopher, Philo of Alexandria (c. 20 BCE to 50 CE). In his *Life of Moses*, Philo glosses Exodus 3:14: '[T]ell them that I am He Who is [*ho on*], that they may learn the difference between what is [*ontos*] and what is not [*mē ontos*], and also the further lesson that no name at all can properly be used of Me, to Whom alone existence [*to einai*] belongs' (I.75).[59]

Philo's interpretation attempts to unify the Hebrew narrative with the Middle Platonist philosophy in which he was trained (Sterling 2014). He sees the divine name in apophatic terms as a marker of God's transcendence above all naming – 'no personal name even can be properly assigned to the truly Existent [*to onti*] ... [God said] I am He that is [*ho on*]', which is equivalent to 'My nature is to be [*to einai*], not to be spoken' (*On the Change of Names* II.11).[60] The theological language of *ho on* and *to on* in Philo echoes Plato's language in the *Timaeus*, where the speaker Timaeus asks: 'what is it that always is [*to on*], but never comes to be, and what is it that comes to be but never is [*on*]?' (27d).[61] For

---

[58] New Revised Standard Version, with Hebrew and Septuagint Greek interpolated.
[59] Trans. (Philo 1935).   [60] Trans. (Philo 1934).   [61] Trans. (Plato 2008).

Philo, the Mosaic name is an answer to this question: the Hebrew God is none other than the Being of Plato's *Timaeus*. He thus adapts the Platonist ontological framework to distinguish Abrahamic Creator and creature: 'God alone has veritable being [*to einai*]. This is why [he is called] "I AM He that is," implying that others lesser than He have not being . . . but exist in semblance only' (*Quod deterius* 160).[62]

As we will see, many BI thinkers in our period follow Philonic lines in their interpretations of the Exodus 3:14 name (Gericke 2012). Indeed, the Exodus text even influenced pagan thinkers outside the Abrahamic traditions (Kooten 2006, 107–85). The *ho on* ascription in Numenius noted earlier (fr. 13) is likely borrowed from the Septuagint (Burnyeat 2006), and in an extraordinary remark apparently directed at the Exodus text, Numenius asks: 'what is Plato but Moses talking Attic?' (fr. 8).[63]

The Christian Tradition

A vast swathe of Christian thinkers in our period endorse some version of BI. The earliest patristic instances tend to share the BB–BI ambiguities of Middle Platonism. Justin Martyr (c. 100–165), for example, combines both languages in a single sentence: 'the very Being [*to on*] who is the cause of everything the mind perceives . . . who is beyond all essence [*on epekeina pases ousia*], who is ineffable and indescribable, who alone is beautiful and good' (*Dial.* chap. 4).[64] Clement of Alexandria (c. 150–215) seems to hedge his position. He argues that 'as, then, [God] is being [*estin ousia*], He is the first principle of the department of action, as He is good, of morals' (*Strom.* 4). He elsewhere states that philosophical inquiry aims at 'the most excellent essence [*ousia*] of all' – apparently a reference to the divine Word – 'and essays to go beyond [*epekeina*] to the God of the universe', implying that the Father is beyond *ousia* (*Strom.* 1).[65] He even suggests that 'God is one, and beyond [*epekeina*] the one and above unity [*monada*] itself' (*Paedagogus* 1).[66] These tensions can perhaps be construed as a principled dimension of Clement's apophatic theology (Hägg 2006, 153–79).

Origen (c. 185–253) is a particularly intriguing case. He laments the difficulty of deciding between a BB and BI position (*Contra Celsum* VI.64).[67] He frequently refers to God in terms of being, often alluding to the Exodus

---

[62] Trans. (Philo 1929).

[63] The remark is cited approvingly in Clement, *Strom.* I.22 and Eusebius, *Praep. evan.* IX.6; see Whittaker (1967). Plotinus explicitly rejects a similar formulation: 'What would [the One] know about itself? "I am" [*ego eimi*]? But it is not [*ouk esti*]!' (*Enn.* VI.7.38).

[64] Trans. (Martyr 2003).   [65] Trans. (Schaff 1885). Cf. *Protrepticus* 88, 117.

[66] Trans. (Schaff 1885), trans. modified.

[67] Trans. (Origen 1953). Quoted as an epigraph to this study.

name – for example, 'in him who truly exists [*uere est*], who said by Moses, *I am who I am* [*Ego sum qui sum*], all things that are have participation' (*De prin.* I.3.6).[68] He contrasts 'He who is' with the 'nothing' and 'non-being' of evil (*In Jo.* 2.92–99). But, elsewhere, he appears to take a BB position, following *Republic* 509b. He speculates that the Trinitarian Logos may be 'being of beings [*ousia ousion*]', while the Father transcends *ousia* (*Contra Celsum* VI.64) and seems to positively endorse the view elsewhere: 'first one apprehends the truth' – which here refers to the Johannine Logos – 'so that in this way he may come to behold the essence [*ousia*], or the power and nature of God beyond the essence [*huperekeina tēs ousias*]' (*In Jo.* 19.37).[69] In a very curious passage, he adapts Plato's language to argue that the Son (not the Father in this instance) transcends 'by' his being, perhaps suggesting that Platonist transcendence may in fact be secured through a special sense of *ousia*,[70] which will be a possibility developed by later BI thinkers. Elsewhere, Origen implies in a passing comment that Christians might freely go either way: 'we affirm that the God of the universe is mind, *or* that He transcends [*epekeina*] mind and being [*ousias*]' (*Contra Celsum* VII.38, my italics). Contemporary interpreters can take more or less sympathetic views of Origen's BB–BI ambiguities, with some seeing them as a blunder[71] and others as principled articulations of compatible claims.[72]

We noted several major Eastern figures in our survey of the BB tradition. One Eastern theologian who is better positioned in the BI tradition is Gregory of Nyssa (c. 335-395). Commenting on Exodus 3, Gregory argues that 'what the great Moses learnt' is that creaturely things do not have 'a real existence', for 'the only reality that truly exists is the one that is above all of them, the cause of all from which everything depends' (*De vita Moysis* II.2.24).[73] God is thus the one primary reality: 'to be totally independent of all else and . . . to be participated in by all, yet to be in no way thereby diminished, that is to be The Really Real [*to ontos on*]' (II.2.25). Gregory identifies the Good with divine Being: 'what really is, is Absolute Good' (*Hom. Eccl.* VII.406.1).[74] He is also careful to affirm that the status of *ontos on* applies equally to all Trinitarian persons, rejecting Eunomius' view that the Father is the 'highest

---

[68] Trans. (Origen 2017). See also Origen's commentaries on Romans 9:2, John 2:13, and 1 Corinthians 1:28.

[69] Trans. (Origen 2006). See also *De martyrio* 47.

[70] *In Jo.* 13.151 – *huperechon ousias*. See Widdicombe (1994, 39–40).

[71] Raoul Mortley (1986, 75): 'the issue of God's relationship with *ousia* . . . is an embarrassment for Origen'.

[72] Peter Widdicombe (1994, 43): 'Origen would not have seen a tension between the statement that God is "he who is" and the statement that God "transcends mind and being." Indeed, it is possible that he thought of both as biblical concepts, the one found in Exodus 3: 14, and the other in Romans 1: 20'.

[73] Trans. (Meredith 2012). [74] Trans. (Gregory of Nyssa 2012).

and most authentic being', in contrast to the Son, 'which exists because of that being and after that being has supremacy over the rest' (*Contra Eun.* I.156).[75]

Gregory is particularly significant in the BI tradition for theorising God's being as positively *infinite*.[76] 'The Divine is by its very nature infinite [*aoriston*], enclosed by no boundary' (*De vita Moysis* IV.2.236). And he replies to Eunomius: 'if he allows that the underlying being is simple and is properly related to itself, let him agree that it has attached to it the attributes of the simple and infinite [*apeiron*]' (*Contra Eun.* I.236). Unlike many BI thinkers thus far, Gregory is unequivocal in his attribution of being to God.

Turning to Latin Western Christians, we find a large majority expressing some version of BI. Augustine (354–430) is a leading example. Despite his frequent praise for Platonist metaphysics, he seems never to be tempted by BB language. Instead, across his works, he makes straightforward ascriptions of being to God using a range of terminology (e.g. *esse, est, ipsum esse, essentia,* etc.).[77] A typical instance occurs in his exposition of Psalm 134:

> [God] said, I AM WHO AM [*ego sum qui sum*] … He set aside all [other] names that could be applied to God and answered that he was called Being Itself [*ipsum esse*], as though that were his name. Thus shall you say, he ordered, HE WHO IS has sent me. His very nature is to be [*est*] … He is true being [*verum esse*], unchangeable being [*incommutabile esse*], and this can be said of him alone. He is being [*Est enim est*], as he is also goodness, the good of all good things. (*En. Ps.* 134.4)[78]

Augustine emphasises immutability as the defining trait of divinity. God is the *idipsum*, the unique 'selfsame': 'you are supremely "the selfsame" [*idipsum*] in that you do not change' (*Conf.* IX.4).[79] For this reason, 'being' in its strict sense can be ascribed only to God: '*Is* is [*esse est*]. True *is*, genuine *is*, real *is* [*uerum esse, sincerum esse, germanum esse*] belongs only to one who does not change' (*Sermo* 7.7).[80] Indeed, *esse* is the most fitting of all descriptions of God:

---

[75] Trans. (Gregory of Nyssa 2018).   [76] See Weedman (2010).

[77] See, for example, *Conf.* VII.10; *De libero arbitrio* III; *De moribus ecclesiae catholicae* I; *De trin.* V-VII; *Sermones* 7, 7; *De vera religione* 18; *De immortalitate animae* XI; *De civitate Dei* VIII.11.

[78] Trans. (Augustine 2004).

[79] Jean-Luc Marion (2012, 301) argues that, because of his 'equivocity of Being' between immutable divine and mutable creaturely being and despite his frequent BI language, Augustine is best seen as a BB thinker who escapes ontotheology. As my remarks on ontotheology at the end of this study will suggest, I am sympathetic to Marion's post-Heideggerian retrieval of the BI tradition. But I think this can be done via analogy, not necessarily equivocity, and this arguably is closer to Augustine's position.

[80] Trans. (Augustine 1990).

> Being [*ipsum esse*] is in the highest and truest sense of the term proper to Him from whom being [*essentia*] derives its name. For what undergoes a change does not retain its own being ... therefore, only that which is not only not changed, but cannot undergo any change at all, can be called being [*esse*] in the truest sense without any scruple. (*De trin.* V.2)[81]

Whereas creatures exist in some particular kind or mode, for Augustine, God 'does not exist merely in some degree [*modo est*] since he is Existence [*sed est est*]' (*Conf.* XIII.31).[82] He thus instructs: 'we ought, then, to love God the Trinity in unity, Father, Son, and Holy Spirit, and this cannot be called anything other than Being Itself [*idipsum esse*]' (*De mor. ecc.* I.14).[83] Augustine's view here, as in many matters, exerts a profound influence on the medieval Latin tradition, and its echo is heard in practically all subsequent BI thinkers in the Latin West.

Moving into the Latin medieval tradition, BI is evident just about everywhere one looks. I will highlight a few principal thinkers here to illustrate the variety of ways that the BI position is articulated in this tradition. Boethius (c. 475–526) describes God as 'substantial Being [*ipsum esse*] and substantial Good and essential Goodness [*ipsum esse bonum*]' (*Opus. sacra* III.149–150).[84] Anselm (1033–1109) uses the language of a 'supreme reality' (*summa res*) (*Reply to Gaunilo* IV), which is 'before and beyond all things [*ultra omnia*]' and 'of all things possesses existence to the highest degree [*maxime omnium habes esse*]' (*Proslogion* XX, III).[85] The Exodus 3:14 text remains a constant point of reference, as when Hildegard of Bingen (1098–1179) remarks: 'it is said "I am who I am" [*Ego sum qui sum*]. And he-who-is [*qui est*] is fullness [*plenitudinem*] itself' (*Letter* 40R).[86] She argues that 'God alone exists [*est*] in and of himself, nor does he receive his being [*esse*] from anything else; rather, any and all creation takes its being [*esse*] from him' (*Div. operum* II.1.14).[87] A BB emphasis on transcending created beings is still often present in the Latin BI context, as in Richard of St Victor (d. 1173): 'divine substance is nothing else than substantial – or better, super-substantial – being. [It is] substantial because it is a reality subsisting in itself; [it is] super-substantial, because this reality is not subordinated to anything' (*De trin.* IV.19).[88]

Moving into the thirteenth century, Albert the Great (c. 1200–1280), citing Avicenna, notes that 'being is more truly ascribed to God than to anything else' (*In Myst. theo.* V.4).[89] He argues that, in the divine first principle, 'because it does not have *esse* from another, *esse* is per se ... "this which it is" [*hoc quod est*] and its *esse* are one' (*De causis et processu* I.1.8).[90] Bonaventure (c. 1217–1274)

---

[81] Trans. (Augustine 2002).   [82] Trans. (Augustine 1991).   [83] Trans. (Augustine 2010).
[84] Trans. (Boethius 1968).   [85] Trans. (Anselm 1979).
[86] Trans. (Hildegard of Bingen 1994).   [87] Trans. (Hildegard of Bingen 2018).
[88] Trans. (Richard of Saint Victor 2011).   [89] Trans. (Albert the Great 1988).
[90] Trans. (Vargas 2013, 634).

argues that *esse* is the primary name of God, for he is 'pure being [*esse purum*], simple being [*esse simpliciter*], and absolute being [*esse absolutum*] . . . the most actual [*actualissimum*], the most perfect, and the supremely one being' (*Itin.* V.5).[91] The first principle is 'most pure and absolute being [*esse purissimum et absolutum*]' and has being 'in an unqualified sense [*simpliciter esse*]' (V.8). Still, in a Dionysian spirit, the *Itinerarium* gives the final word to the name of *Bonum*: 'just as being itself [*ipsum esse*] is the foundational principle' for knowing divine attributes, 'so the good [*ipsum bonum*] is the most basic foundation for our contemplation of the emanations [of the Trinitarian persons]' (VI.1).[92]

Reaching a little beyond our stated historical period, BI themes are evident in later women theologians. Catherine of Siena (1347–1380) states, in the divine voice, 'Know that no one can escape my hands, for I am who I am [*Ego sum qui sum*], whereas you have no being at all [*non es*]' (*Dialogue* 18).[93] And Julian of Norwich (1342-c. 1416), writing in the Middle English vernacular, praises 'oure hye fader, almighty God, which is [beyng], he knew us and loved us fro before ony time' (*Revelation of Love* chap. 59).[94]

The Islamic-Arabic Tradition

We noted earlier that some Islamic thinkers hold a BB position (e.g. al-Sijistani). However, the majority hold BI views in our period, even while a creative and subtle inheritance of Neoplatonist ideas is evident across the tradition (D'Ancona 2011).

Some of the most important texts for Islamic BI thinking emerge in ninth-century Baghdad. Al-Kindi (c. 800–870), often celebrated as the first philosopher in the Arabic tradition, freely attributes being terminology to God: he is 'the true Being [*al-anniyya al-haqq*] who has not, and never will be, non-being [*lays*], who has always been, and always will be, being [*'ays*]' (*On the Proximate Agent Cause* I.1.215).[95] Probably more important than Kindi's own views are the positions developed by scholars in the 'circle of al-Kindi' (Endress 1997), who translated/adapted Platonist texts and ideas into a new Arabic linguistic and religious context, often with Christian scholars contributing to the work. An especially important set of texts for our purposes is the Arabic *Plotiniana*, which are based on passages from Plotinus.[96] In the longest of these texts, the so-called *Theology of Aristotle*, which in reality is composed

[91] Trans. (Bonaventure 2002).
[92] Cf. Peperzak (1998). J. G. Bougerol judged that Bonaventure was 'without a doubt the most Dionysian mind of the Middle Ages' – see Tobon (2022).
[93] Trans. (Noffke 1980).   [94] Watson and Jenkins (2006).
[95] Trans. (Pormann and Adamson 2012).
[96] Translations of Arabic *Plotiniana* texts in this section are from Adamson (2002b, 124–37).

of selections from the *Enneads*, the first cause is described as 'the First Being
[*al-anniyya al-ula*] . . . the Creator, the Maker, exalted be His name' (I.47). It is
'one and simple, originating the simple things all at once, through being alone
[*bi-annihi faqat*]' (X.175) and is 'the thing existing truly in act . . . he is pure act
[*al-mahd*]' (III.47). The *Sayings of the Greek Sage* similarly argues that the First
Originator 'has no shape [*hilya*] and no particular inherent form . . . He is only
being [*anniyya faqat*], having no attribute suitable to Him' (I.10).

Another important text is the *Discourse on the Pure Good*, sometimes called
the Arabic *De causis*, which adapts passages from Proclus' *Elements of
Theology* and became enormously influential in its subsequent Latin version,
the *Book of Causes* (*Liber de causis*). It describes God as the pure being (*al-
anniyya mahda*, prop. 4) and contrasts Intellect, which 'possesses formal
adornment because it is being [*anniyya*] and form', with the First Cause,
which either 'has no formal adornment because 'It is only being [*anniyya
faqat*]' or, if we are forced to speak of form, then 'Its formal adornment is
infinite and Its individual nature is the Pure Good' (prop. 8).[97]

The Arabic *Plotiniana* and *Procleana* thus use Neoplatonic sources to arrive
at positions that sound very un-Neoplatonic. In depicting God as first being,
being alone, pure being, and so on, these Arabic texts depart from the 'One
beyond being' in Plotinus and Proclus, and they do it in the very act of
translating core BB key texts (D'Ancona 2023). The result is a novel adaptation
of Neoplatonist metaphysics into an Arabic–Abrahamic–monotheistic conceptual context.

The influence of this framework is evident in subsequent Islamic thinkers,
such as al-Farabi (c. 870–950) who construes God as the highest existence
(*mawjud*) and the cause of existence (*wujud*), which enjoys 'the most elevated
rank of perfect existence' and 'is different in substance from everything else'
(*Perfect State* 1.1–2).[98]

A major inheritor of this tradition is Avicenna (980–1037), usually regarded
as the greatest Islamic thinker in our period. Avicenna frequently refers to God
in ontological terms, especially with his preferred description, Necessary
Existent (*wajib al-wujud*). An especially illuminating text is Book VIII of the
Metaphysics, part of his magnum opus, *The Healing* (*Kitāb al-Shifā*).[99] Here
Avicenna states that there is 'something whose existence is necessary . . . [and
this] Necessary Existent is one, nothing sharing with Him in His rank . . . He is
the principle of the necessitation of the existence of everything' (VIII.4.1). He
explains: 'the primary attribute of the Necessary Existent consists in his being

---

[97] Trans. (Adamson 2002a; Taylor 2020). [98] Trans. (Walzer 1985).
[99] Trans. (Avicenna 2005).

"a that" [*annahu*] and an existent [*mawjud*]' (VIII.7.12). This account of God as the Necessary Existent relies on Avicenna's distinctive metaphysics of essence (*al-dat, mahiyya*) and existence (*al-inniyya, anniyya*) (Lizzini 2003), which, roughly speaking, distinguishes between *what* something is (its essence, nature, quiddity, and thingness) and the fact *that* something is (its existence and realisation). In the background here, in addition to his Arabic influences, is probably Aristotle's old distinction between the question of 'what' a thing is and 'if' or 'that' a thing is.[100] Avicenna holds that all beings have an essence, but their existence is contingent – they might not exist – and they must receive existence from another. The single exception is God, whose existence is necessary and a source of being for creatures. Thus, Avicenna uses essence/existence and contingency/necessity to articulate a distinctive version of the BI position: God is identified with being in the sense that he is *necessary being*, the unique Necessary Existent who gives existence to the essences of contingent creatures.

Despite his novelties, Avicenna is evidently still working in the tradition of Arabic Neoplatonism discussed earlier. In particular, he identifies the Necessary Existent with 'pure being' (*mugarrad al-wugud*) and 'thatness' (*anniyya*):

> [T]here is no quiddity for the Necessary Existent other than its being the Necessary Existent. And this is 'thatness' [*al-anniyya*] (VIII.4.9).

> The First, hence, has no quiddity [*mahiyyata*]. Those things possessing quiddities have existence emanate on them from Him. He is pure existence [*mugarrad al-wugud*] with the condition of negating privation and all other description of Him. (VIII.4.13)

Avicenna thus appears to appropriate the Arabic *De causis*' notion of a first principle of pure being (*anniyya faqat*) (Bertolacci 2020; D'Ancona 2000). As the *De causis* argues that the first cause has no form 'because It is only being [*anniyya faqat*]', so Avicenna argues that God has no quiddity/essence because he is only *anniyya* or pure existence.[101] His BI position can thus be seen as continuing the Arabic reworking of the Plotinian 'One beyond being' into a God of 'pure being', while retaining a basic BB insight: Avicenna's first principle, as pure existence, is without essence and therefore beyond essence, like Plato's Good.[102]

---

[100] See *Posterior Analytics* II; *De Interpretatione* XI; *Metaphysics* V.5 and V.7.

[101] Avicenna elsewhere speaks positively about a divine essence/quiddity and determining his settled view is complicated (Rosheger 2002).

[102] Indeed, Avicenna's student al-Marzuban (d. 1066) reports that, for Avicenna, 'the closest we can come to grasping [God's] true nature is by thinking of Him as being per se' but because 'He is intrinsically the very cause of being ... His essence should be regarded as beyond-being [*fawq al-wujud*]' (Kars 2019, 91).

Islamic thinkers after Avicenna carry on intense debates about theological ontology, but the Avicennian framework tends to set the terms of discussion. For instance, Al-Ghazali's (1058–1111) *On the Incoherence of the Philosophers* and Averroes' (1126–1198) response, *The Incoherence of the Incoherence*, dispute the relationship between God's quiddity (*mahiyya*) and existence (*wujud*).[103] While they disagree with each other and Avicenna over various modal, linguistic, and metaphysical issues, Ghazali and Averroes assume the basic Avicennian view that God is the Necessary Existent.

The Jewish Tradition

We have already noted one Jewish thinker central to the BI tradition, namely Philo. Other important Jewish BI thinkers emerge in the medieval period, working in the wake of some Islamic figures we have just noted and in some cases sharing their Arabic linguistic and intellectual milieu (Harvey 2004).

The pre-eminent figure is, of course, Maimonides (1138–1204). Maimonides frequently attributes being (*wujud, anniyya*) to God. Following Avicenna, he construes God as the Necessary Existent (*wajib al-wujud*) (e.g. *Guide* II.2) and argues that 'we are only able to apprehend the fact that He is [*anniyya*] and cannot apprehend His quiddity [*mahiyya*]' (I.58). It is God's uncaused status that makes his existence necessary: 'as for that which has no cause for its existence, there is only God … His existence is necessary. Accordingly, His existence is identical with His essence and His true reality, and His essence is His existence' (I.57). Like Philo and other Jews before him, he interprets the Exodus 3:14 name in an ontological fashion: '*I am that I am*. This is a name deriving from the verb *to be* [*hayah*], which signifies existence, for *hayah* indicates the notion: he was … [This leads to] the view that there is a necessarily existent thing' (*Guide* I.63).

One complication in Maimonides' BI position, however, is his famously apophatic view of theological speech and its application to 'being' talk about God. He proposes: 'the term "existent" is predicated of Him, may He be exalted, and of everything that is other than He, in a purely equivocal sense. Similarly the terms "knowledge," "power," "will," and "life"' (I.56; cf. I.35). He explains: 'the qualificative attributions ascribed to Him and the meaning of the attributions known to us have nothing in common in any respect or in any mode; these attributions have in common only the name and nothing else' (I.56). This starkly apophatic view might encourage us to align Maimonides more with the BB tradition. If ontological talk does not attribute being to God in any true or substantial sense, then perhaps God is, in the end, beyond being in a Plotinian

---

[103] See Al-Ghazali (2002) and Averroes (2016).

fashion. However, alongside claims about equivocation, Maimonides appears to set apart the biblical Tetragrammaton YHWH – which he seems to align with the Exodus 3:14 name in *Guide* I.62–63 (Lobel 2020) – as the sole exception to the rule of equivocation. YHWH 'has been originated without any derivation . . . and for this reason it is called the *articulated name*. This means that this name gives a clear unequivocal indication of His essence' (*Guide* I.61). What is the meaning of the exceptional name, YHWH? Maimonides acknowledges that the linguistic origins of the term are mysterious but suggests that 'perhaps [YHWH] indicates the notion of a necessary existence [*wajib al-wujud*] according to the [Hebrew] language' (I.61). He later confirms this: 'all names are derived or are used equivocally, as *Rock* and others similar to it', excepting only YHWH, which signifies 'simple existence and nothing else. Now absolute existence implies that He shall always be, I mean He who is necessarily existent' (I.63). Though there are debates around Maimonides' view of the Tetragrammaton (Segal 2021), it gives us sufficient reason to count him as a BI thinker, even with his doctrine of equivocity.

Many Jewish thinkers in our period after Maimonides take BI positions. For instance, Gersonides (1288–1344) resists the extremities of the Rambam's apophaticism and argues that 'such terms as "exists," "one," "essence" . . . are said of God by priority and of others beside Him by posteriority. This is so because His existence, oneness, and essence belong to Him by virtue of Himself' (*Wars* III.3).[104] We can therefore affirm that 'God is more properly called "existent" and "one" than anything else', as is confirmed by the Mosaic name, '*I am what I am*, which is a term signifying being and existence'.[105] Ibn Gabirol (eleventh century) describes God as first being (*primum esse*) and 'only being' (*esse tantum*) (*Fons Vitae* V.32, V.24).[106] And Falaquera's thirteenth-century Hebrew adaptation of the *Fons Vitae* argues that 'the Most High is existence not possessing quiddity, quality, or quarity [i.e. final causation]'.[107]

As we noted in our BB survey, the Sethian Gnostics (second–third century) are arguably part of the Jewish tradition, and some BI themes are evident in their enigmatic texts (Corrigan and Rasimus 2013). The *Apocryphon of John* states that the first principle 'is not at all someone who exists [*etshoop*], but he is something superior [*ouhōb efsotp*] to them, not as being superior, but as being

---

[104] Trans. (Gersonides 2008).

[105] Cf. *Wars* III.3: 'God is that which disposes all other things to be substances, because he gives them their substantiality. Hence, he is more properly called substance'.

[106] Ibn Gabirol (2005).

[107] Trans. (Shem Tov b. Joseph Falaquera and Solomon ibn Gabirol 2008). For the Hebrew terminology for 'existence' (*haluth*) in the background here, see Altman and Stern (2010, 13n2).

himself [*epōf emmin emmof pe*]' (Berlin Codex 24).[108] And *Allogenes* argues that 'he is an entity insofar as he exists . . . although he acts without Mind or Life or Existence or Non-existence, incomprehensibly' (XI.61 NH Codex).[109]

The Act of Being

To bring our survey of the BI tradition to its most renowned contributor, Thomas Aquinas, we need to retrace our historical steps. At some point in late antiquity, a novel notion of being as *act* emerged, opening new possibilities for thinking about existence as a pure, undetermined, and infinite activity. In this section, we will trace the emergence of this 'act of being' concept, which eventually informs Aquinas' celebrated account of God as *ipsum esse subsistens*.

The Anonymous Commentary

Our first port of call is an obscure and fragmentary text known today as the *Anonymous Commentary on Plato's Parmenides* (Bechtle 1999). Discovered in the 1870s and only partially preserved, it has received considerable attention following the ground-breaking work of Pierre Hadot, who attributed it to Porphyry (Hadot 1968). The authorship remains contested, with alternatives including second-century Middle Platonists, Sethian Gnostics, or a post-Plotinian figure (Clark 2017; Turner and Corrigan 2011a). Hadot's position probably has majority support today. For the purposes of this study, we need not take a view and will remain agnostic regarding authorship.

In fragment V, the Anonymous Commentator confronts a difficulty in the second hypothesis of Plato's *Parmenides* (142b-155e). Like some Platonists noted in our BB survey, the Commentator holds that there are two Ones, mapping on to different elements of the *Parmenides* discussion. According to the Commentator, Plato holds that the second One 'participates in substance [*ousias*]'. But how is this possible, when the first principle is supposed to be 'beyond substance', as the *Republic* 509b text has it? In what being does the second One participate?

> Behold whether Plato does not seem to speak in riddles, because the One, which is 'beyond substance' and beyond being [*epekeina ousias kai ontos*] on the one hand is neither being nor substance nor activity [*energeia*], but on the other hand acts and is itself pure act [*energein katharon*], so that it is also the

---

[108] Trans. (Wisse and Waldstein 1995, 186). John Turner (2001, 504): the Sethian Gnostic first principle, 'although strictly beyond existence, he has a "non-being existence," a pre-existing or prefigurative or paradigmatic existence from which actual Existence derives'. There are similarities here with the *Anonymous Commentary*, which we will discuss in detail in the following.

[109] Trans. (Turner 2001, 506).

being before being [*to einai to pro tou ontos*]. By participating in it the other
One receives a derivative being [*to einai*], which indeed is to participate in
being. Thus, being is double [*ditton to einai*]: the one exists prior to being
[*ontos*], the other is brought forth from the One which is beyond, the absolute
being [*einai to apoluton*] and as it were 'idea' of being [*idea tou ontos*]. (frag.
V)[110]

To solve the puzzle of two Ones, the Commentator here splits his notion of
being in two: 'being is double'. The being of the first One is absolute *einai*
and pure *energeia*; it is *einai* before *ontos*; it is beyond *ousia* and *ontos*; it
serves as the *idea* of *ontos*. The being of the second One, on the other hand, is
derivative and participated *ontos*. This innovative 'double being' structure
integrates the Aristotelian notion of act (*energeia*) with being so that the first
principle's pure being is identified with pure activity (*energein katharon*).
The Anonymous Commentator thus proposes a new sense of 'being' as
unrestricted and undetermined activity, articulated with the infinitive *to
einai*, to indicate action abstracted from any particular subject. As Jean-
François Courtine observes, 'we must indeed emphasize the boldness of the
[Commentator] . . . this entails a profound redefinition of being (*to einai* = *to
energein*), taken in an active sense, and rigorously distinguished from what
exists' (2014, 303).

Victorinus

The Commentator's double being framework appears to be reflected in the Latin
writings of the Christian thinker, Victorinus (290–364), and it is very likely that
there is direct influence (Bradshaw 2004, 108–14; Cooper 2016; Hadot
1968).[111] While Victorinus can sometimes speak in straightforward BB
style,[112] in an important passage, he clarifies that there is a peculiar sense of
'being' attributable to his first principle, which in Victorinus' Trinitarian context now refers to the Father:

> Before the existent [*on*] and before the Logos, there is that force and that
> power of being [*exsistendi*] that is designated by the word 'to be' [*esse*], in
> Greek *to einai*. This very 'to be' [*ipsum esse*] must be taken under two modes,
> one that is universal and originally original, and from it comes the 'to be'
> [*esse*] for all others; and according to another mode, all others have 'to be'

---

[110] Trans. (Bradshaw 2004, 103).

[111] An additional line of influence here may run through the Sethian Gnostic treatises (Tomassi
2022; Turner 2007).

[112] For example, *Adv. Cand.* 13.7: '[God] is above every existent [*on*] and the truly existents [*ton
onton*] . . . because he is above existents, he has nothing from existents. God is therefore
nonexistent [*mē on*]' (trans. (Victorinus 1981)).

[*esse*], this is the 'to be' [*esse*] of all those which come after God, genera or species or other things of this kind. But the first 'to be' [*esse*] is so unparticipated that it cannot even be called one or alone, but rather, by preeminence, before the one, before the alone, beyond simplicity, preexistence rather than existence, universal of all universals, infinite [*infinitum*], unlimited [*interminatum*] ... [This is] 'to be' in itself [*ipsum esse*], 'to live' in itself, not to be something [*aliquid esse*] or to live something. Whence, it is not existent [*on*]. For the existent [*on*] is something determined, intelligible, knowable. (*Ad. Arium* IV.19)[113]

Victorinus presents here a Latin adaptation of the Commentator's double being structure. The first divine being is *esse* – a term which Victorinus explicitly notes is a rendering of *to einai* – abstracted from particularity. It is *ipsum esse* in an infinite, undetermined, and unrestricted way; it is not particularised, not to-be-something (*aliquid esse*) but to-be itself and as such (*ipsum esse*). This *esse* is not determinate, as is the case in the *esse* of particular existing beings (*on*). Like the Commentator, Victorinus also identifies this infinitive *esse* with action. As he explains elsewhere: 'this "to be" itself [*ipsum esse*], which is the Father, by the very fact that it is "to be" [*esse*] is to act [*agere*] and to work [*operari*]. For up there "to be" [*esse*] does not differ from "to act" [*operari*]' (*Ad Cand.* 19). Thus, the Father is 'at once "to be" [*esse*] and "to act" [*operari*]'; he is 'first act [*actio*] and first existence [*exsistentia*]' (*Adv. Arium* I.33). Victorinus' Trinitarian theology thus aims at 'identifying Being with Action, referring to it as Power of Being or Substantial Action' (Clark 1972). David Bradshaw sees this Latin construal of being-as-act as Victorinus' major conceptual advance:

In effect we find in Victorinus a further specification of the *energein katharon* of the Anonymous Commentary. This *energein* now turns out to be *esse*, the unlimited and uncircumscribed being of the Father, from which is derived all the limited and circumscribed being (*on*) found in the Son. Such *esse* is anything but 'being' conceived as a static condition of existence; it is a kind of inwardly directed activity, containing implicitly life and intelligence as well as existence. (Bradshaw 2004, 114)

With the Anonymous Commentator and Victorinus, then, we find a combination of Aristotle's notion of the prime mover as pure intellectual act (*energein*) with the Platonist notion of a first principle beyond being (*epekeina ousias*), which is used to re-imagine the Platonic transcendence of *ousia/ontos* in terms of an undetermined, infinite, and divine act of being (*to einai* or *esse*). With the Commentator and Victorinus, we therefore hear the first Greek and Latin articulations of divine being in the infinitive, unqualified sense of *ipsum esse* and *actus purus*, which Aquinas

---

[113] Trans. (Victorinus 1981).

will later conceptualise with such sophistication.[114] That this idea emerges first in two thorough-going Platonists is an irony that will not be lost on readers of Étienne Gilson.[115]

Transmission to the Scholastics

Though it is highly probable that the Anonymous Commentator's notion of pure act *einai* exerts a long-distance influence on Aquinas, the lines of transmission are hard to draw. One likely route for the Anonymous Commentator's notion of double being into the Middle Ages is through Boethius.[116] Boethius was familiar with some of Victorinus' writings, likely including the *Adversus Arium* texts cited earlier. In his *De hebdomadibus*, Boethius distinguishes between *esse* and *id quod est* (what it is):

> Being [*esse*] and a concrete thing [*id quod est*] are different. Simple being [*ipsum esse*] awaits manifestation [*nondum est*], but a thing [*id quod est*] is and exists as soon as it has received the form which gives it being [*forma esse*]. (*Opus. sacra* III prop. 2)

Boethius' *esse*/*id quod est* distinction appears to correspond with Victorinus' *esse*/*on* distinction. In each case, being has two senses: the first is an indeterminate *esse* and the second is *esse* determined by a form to become a concrete being: '*on* is *esse* determined by a certain form' (Victorinus); *ipsum esse* is 'not yet' being (*nondum est*), but *id quod est* exists upon receiving a form (Boethius). For his part, Boethius is describing ontology in general in this passage, not Trinitarian theological ontology, but it is possible that this sense of *esse* is in play also in his descriptions elsewhere of God as transcendent *ipsum esse*.[117]

Another possible transmission route for the Commentator's double being is the Arabic tradition. Richard Taylor, following French scholarship,[118] argues that the language of pure being (*anniyya faqat*) and pure act (*al-fil al-mahd*) in the Arabic *Plotiniana* and *Procleana* appears to echo the Commentary's *energein katharon* and *to einai* (Taylor 1998). He suggests that the Commentator's novel theological ontology thus passes into the Latin West via translations of Avicenna and the *De causis*. Some are not convinced – Christine D'Ancona, for instance, argues that the precise distinction between *einai* and *on* is not present in the Arabic sources and prefers a Pseudo-Dionysian source for the Arabic pure

---

[114] Mary Clark (2007, 286): 'Victorinus seems to have been the first to call the Judaeo-Christian God *Esse* in a positive and infinite sense'.

[115] We will discuss Gilson's neo-Thomistic allergy to Platonism in the following.

[116] Pierre Hadot (1963) suggested this, and several scholars have advanced the view, for example, Bradshaw (1999), Brock (2007), Corrigan (1984), and Rosheger (2001).

[117] See citations in survey treatment of Boethius above. See also Gersh (1986, 679–83).

[118] Thillet (1971); Pines (1971).

being language.[119] Others support Taylor's proposal – Michael Chase even suggests that 'the most striking common feature' of the Greek, Latin, and Arabic traditions, namely 'the description of the First Principle as Being (Greek *to einai*, Latin *esse*, Arabic *anniyya*)', may emerge from a shared 'philosophical *koinê*' proposed single-handedly by Porphyry in the *Parmenides Commentary* (Chase 2020, 2022, 476). We cannot adjudicate the debate here, but we can confidently say that the notion of pure being and pure act developed by Aquinas has prior analogues (if not sources) in the Arabic tradition.

A third possible route to Latin scholasticism is through Augustine. Sarah Klittenic Wear argues that Augustine's Trinitarian metaphysics, particularly as expressed in his exposition of John 5:19, reflects Victorinus' account of *esse* and *potentia* in Father and Son and, therefore, also the Anonymous Commentator's account of *einai/energeia* and *dunamis* in the First and Second One.[120] Mary Clark suggests that Augustine's treatment of divine substance in *De trinitate* V.2 – where he argues that 'Being [*ipsum esse*] is in the highest and truest sense of the term proper to Him from whom being [*essentia*] derives its name' – reflects Victorinus' view of the Father's infinite *esse*.[121] Some scholars doubt a significant influence on Augustine in this area.[122] If the link with Augustine is in fact plausible, then we can see Augustine[123] and Victorinus[124] as working at the same task of 'flattening' or 'telescoping' Platonist hypostases in conformity with emerging Christian orthodoxy, according to which the three Trinitarian hypostases are ontologically coequal.[125] This flattening of hypostases, which is carried on in other patristic contexts too,[126] shifts the crucial 'ontological difference' from a distinction between first and second hypostases in the pagan Platonists to an Abrahamic distinction between divine and created being. Such Christian revisions to Platonist frameworks do not deter patristic theologians from sometimes happily acknowledging affinities between Christian and Platonist triple hypostases (Radde-Gallwitz 2020).

---

[119] D'Ancona-Costa (1995, 121–54); D'Ancona (2011).

[120] Wear (2011). See also the related discussion in Byers (2022).   [121] Clark (2007, 290).

[122] See, for example, Bradshaw (2004, 114–15) and Hadot (1968).

[123] David Bradshaw (2008, 240): '[in Augustine] the greatest change from Plotinus consists not in collapsing the distinction of hypostases, but in rejecting the hierarchical ranking that allows the One and Intellect to differ in respect to being, unity, and intelligibility'.

[124] Mary Clark (2009, 92): 'Victorinus has effectively eliminated subordinationism within the Platonian triad … action was then seen to be subsistent, substantial, and capable of distinguishing the Three Persons'.

[125] The Trinitarian 'flattening' can be compared / contrasted with Porphyry's 'telescoping of hypostases', which so disturbs later Neoplatonists (Lloyd 1970, 287–93).

[126] For instance, in the Cappadocians – see Lilla (1997, 154–67). Indeed, Rowan Williams argues that the whole Arian controversy is in part a dispute about whether and how this flattening should proceed (Williams 2002, 181–268).

Thomas Aquinas

With this genealogy of the 'act of being' in mind, we now turn to Thomas Aquinas (1225–1274), the pre-eminent BI thinker of the Middle Ages. There are several aspects to note in Aquinas' account of God and being.[127] First are linguistic issues. Aquinas gives a privileged place to 'being' in his treatments of the divine names.[128] He sees the Exodus 3:14 name as the 'most proper' name of God, more proper even than 'Good', because the name 'does not signify form, but simply existence itself' (*ST* I.13.11 *resp.*).[129] With other divine names 'some mode of substance is determined', but *qui est* is indeterminate and so it best indicates the divine infinity. The attribution of being follows Aquinas' doctrine of analogy: perfections are attributed to God in neither a univocal nor a purely equivocal sense but 'in an analogous sense [*secundum analogiam*]' (*ST* I.13.5 *resp.*). Thus, 'being' and other perfections such as 'good' and 'life' are truly attributed to God, even if God's transcendence entails that we say more than we know when we make such predications.[130] For perfections 'pre-exist … in Him in a more eminent way than can be understood or signified' (*ST* I.13.2 ad 2).

These linguistic considerations map onto Aquinas' metaphysics of divine causation: perfections are attributed 'according to the relation of a creature to God as its principle and cause wherein all perfections of things pre-exist excellently' (*ST* I.13.5 *resp.*). Aquinas deploys Platonist metaphysics of participation to explain this structure:

> [A]ll beings apart from God are not their own being [*esse*], but are beings by participation [*participant esse*]. Therefore it must be that all things which are diversified by the diverse participation of being, so as to be more or less perfect, are caused by one First Being [*primo ente*], Who *is* most perfectly [*perfectissime est*]. (*ST* I.44.1 *resp.*)[131]

Aquinas elsewhere puts this in terms of 'having' *esse* versus 'being' *esse*: 'that which has existence [*habet esse*] but is not existence, is a being [*ens*] by participation' (ST I.3.4 *resp.*), but unlike creatures, the first cause 'does not have participated being [*esse participatum*], but it itself is pure being [*esse purum*]' (*In De causis* prop. 9).[132] Whereas the existence of all creatures is the

---

[127] There is a vast literature relevant to Aquinas' account of God and being. Useful recent work in English includes: Velde (1995); O'Rourke (1992); Cullen and Harkins (2019).

[128] See *In Sent.* I d. 8 q. 1 a. 1; *In Div. nom.* V.11 *De potentia dei* 7.5; *ST* I.13.11.

[129] Trans. (Aquinas 1920).

[130] Cf. Denys Turner (2004, 185–6): 'Of course, we could not know what it means to say that God is "pure act," *ipsum esse subsistens* … [these phrases are] intended to mark out with maximum clarity and precision the locus of the divine incomprehensibility'.

[131] Trans. modified.   [132] Trans. (Aquinas 1996).

effect of a prior cause, God is 'just existence [*esse tantum*]' and is the 'cause of existing [*causa essendi*]' in all beings (*De ente* 3).[133] The distinction of essence and existence – a version of which we encountered in Avicenna – functions for Aquinas in a similar way. Every creature is composed of an essence (*essentia*), which determines 'what' it is, and a distinct existence (*esse*), by which it is a real and existing thing. God is the single instance in which essence and existence are identical, and so the 'what' of God is simply his own existence:

> For as the sun possesses light by its nature, and as the air is enlightened by
> sharing the sun's nature; so God alone is Being in virtue of His own Essence
> [*est ens per essentiam*], since His Essence is His existence [*essentia est suum
> esse*]; whereas every creature has being by participation [*est ens participa-
> tive*], so that its essence is not its existence. (*ST* I.104.1 *resp.*)

One perhaps surprising upshot of this account of participation and essence/existence is that, for Aquinas, God is 'beyond being' in a sense strikingly similar to Platonist formulations. For Aquinas, God lies *outside* the realm of beings and being – he cannot be 'in the box' of being. God 'must be understood as existing outside of the order of beings [*extra ordinem entium existens*] as a cause producing the whole of being [*totum ens*] and all its differences' (*In Peri herm.* I.14.22).[134] He is the principle and source of all existence (*fontale principium totius esse*) (*SCG* I.68); he 'is not contained in the genus of substance but is above all substance [*supra omnem substantiam*]' (*De pot.* 7.3 ad 4);[135] he is outside the 'common being' (*ens commune, esse commune*) shared by creatures;[136] he is outside being *qua* being, which is studied in the discipline of metaphysics, as its principle and cause (*In Boet. De trin.* V.4). Indeed, a salutary apophatic theology 'will remove even this very being [*ipsum esse*] from Him, according as it is in creatures' (*In Sent.* I.8.1).[137]

Because God is outside creaturely being in these ways, Aquinas is even willing to countenance language of God's 'non-existence'. Responding to Dionysius' claim that 'God is not something existing [*non est existens*]; but He is rather super-existence [*supra existentia*]', Aquinas responds: 'God is not said to be not existing as if He did not exist at all, but because He exists above all that exists [*est supra omne existens*]; inasmuch as He is His own existence' (*ST* I.12.1 ad 3). Or again: 'God, since he is the cause of all existing things, himself is nothing of existing things [*nihil est existentium*], not as though failing from

---

[133] Trans. (Aquinas 1968).   [134] Trans. (Aquinas 1962)   [135] Trans. (Aquinas 1952).

[136] *In Div. nom.* V.II.660: 'God himself is not of being [*non ipse Deus est esse*], that is, of common being [*esse communis*] itself ... all existing things are contained under common being itself [*ipso esse communi*], yet God is not, but rather common being is contained under his virtue'. Cf. *ST* I.3.4 ad 2; *SCG* I.26.

[137] Trans. (Aquinas 1997).

being [*deficiens ab essendo*], but supereminently segregated from all things' (*In Div. nom.* I.3.83).[138] The same analysis that we suggested for BB thinkers applies also to Aquinas: God in a sense does not exist, not because he is less than being but because he is somehow more than being.

Lastly, and most importantly for his account of God and being, Aquinas inherits and advances the 'act of being' tradition that we have been tracing in this section. He systematically applies the Aristotelian act–potency framework to the most basic 'act' of all: *esse*, the act of existing. 'Existence [*esse*]', he argues, 'denotes a kind of act [*actum*], since a thing is said to exist not through being in potency, but through being in act' (*SCG* I.22).[139] Existence (*esse*) should then be thought of more as an action or activity, rather than property, fact, or state of affairs. Existence is a verb: the word 'is' (*est*) 'signifies to be in act [*actu esse*], and therefore signifies in the mode of a verb' (*In Peri. herm.* lect. 5). Grammatically, *esse* is the Latin infinitive 'to be': as a runner performs the act of running ('to run'), so a being (*ens*) performs the act of existing ('to be', *esse*) (*In De hebd.* lect. 2).[140] This 'act' character of existence establishes *esse*'s central place in Aquinas' metaphysics – it is 'the actuality of all acts [*actualitas omnium actuum*], and therefore, the perfection of all perfections' (*De pot.* q. 7 a. 2 ad 9).[141]

Aquinas' understanding of *esse* as act informs his theological ontology. 'In God there is nothing of potency ... he is pure act [*purum actum*]' (*SCG* I.22); the first cause 'is infinite act [*actus infinitus*], as having in itself the entire fullness of being [*essendi plenitudinem*], not contracted to any generic or specific nature' and therefore not 'limited [*finiretur*]' by a specific nature (*De spir. creat.* 1 *resp.*).[142] The Anonymous Commentator's pure act *einai* and Victorinus' indeterminate *esse*, which is not 'to-be something' (*aliquid esse*) but 'to-be itself' (*ipsum esse*), echoes here in Aquinas' divine act of being. And it is reflected in Aquinas' most celebrated description of God, *ipsum esse subsistens*: '[God] is supremely being [*maxime ens*], inasmuch as His being is not determined by any nature to which it is adjoined; since He is being itself, subsistent [*ipsum esse subsistens*], absolutely undetermined [*omnibus modis indeterminatum*]' (*ST* I.11.4 *resp.*).

The angelic doctor thus develops a sophisticated rendition of BI theological ontology, integrating Platonist transcendence and participation, Aristotelian act–potency, and Avicennian essence–existence with a distinctive 'double being' notion of divine *esse* as infinite, undetermined, and plenitudinous act.

---

[138] Trans. (Aquinas 2022).   [139] Trans. (Aquinas 1955).   [140] Cf. *In Sent.* I d. 19, q. 2, a. 2.
[141] For the importance of this theme across Aquinas' philosophy and theology, see Wippel (2000).
[142] Trans. (Aquinas 1949).

The Logic of BI

As with the BB tradition, we can identify some core convictions and arguments that tend to underlie BI positions in our period.

Beyond Knowledge and Language

An apophaticism comparable to that of the BB tradition is present through the BI tradition.[143] While there are different emphases and different degrees of apophatic rigor across individual thinkers, this theme is a striking commonality across the two traditions. Gregory of Nyssa, for instance, argues that 'the Really Real ... is inaccessible to our understanding' (*Life of Moses*, IV.2.235). Augustine sets down the rule that 'if you can comprehend it, it is not God' (*Sermo* 117.5), and Maimonides argues that 'none but He Himself can apprehend what He is' for 'He is hidden from us ... just as the sun is hidden to eyes that are too weak to apprehend it' (*Guide* I.59). The identification of God with being is plainly not inimical to the apophatic impulse. One common BI variation on this theme is to emphasise that God, as *esse*, is intelligible to himself and knows himself, even while remaining beyond the comprehension of creatures. Thus, according to Aquinas: 'God, whose being is infinite ... is infinitely knowable. Now no created intellect can know God infinitely' (*ST* I.12.7 s.c.). The Parmenidean being–thinking link therefore tends to impinge on the BI tradition in a different way – divine being is now thinkable but not by *creaturely* thinkers – though with the same outcome as in the BB tradition: God exceeds our minds and words.

Not a Being among Beings

Like the BB tradition, BI thinkers are committed to the view that God is not an existing thing in the set of existing things. We noted this in detail in our consideration of Aquinas, and the point is often emphasised by Thomists today. For instance, Ralph McInerny: 'God is not a being among beings, a kind of being, a thing for whom to exist is measured by a determinate form different from other determinate forms'.[144] Other BI thinkers express comparable views. Albert, for instance, argues that 'God is not categorized with other things that exist [*existentibus*], as if he formed a class with them' (*In Myst. theo.* 821A).[145] Others state the same idea but reverse the comparison: God is the one true being, and creatures are outsiders to the realm of (divine) being. For

---

[143] See, for example, Mortley (1986), Carabine (1992a), and Rocca (2004).

[144] See McInerny (2012, 253). See also, for example, Davies (1996) and Perl (2014, 158–61). For a defense of 'a being' language about God from a Thomistic point of view, see Stump (2018).

[145] Trans. (Albert the Great 1988).

Augustine, God's 'very nature is to be [*est*]', while creatures are 'as though they had no being ... compared with him they do not exist' (*En. Ps.* 134.4). Anselm argues that only God 'exist[s] in an unqualified sense and perfectly and absolutely, whereas all other things nearly do not exist at all, and barely do exist' (*Mono.* 28).[146] For Philo, creatures 'exist in semblance only' (*Quod deterius* 160). Palamas puts it both ways in a single sentence: God 'is not a being [*on estin*], if others are beings; and if he is a being [*on*], the others are not beings' (*Capita* 78). These two rhetorical routes arrive at the same philosophical point: God and beings do not lie on a common ontological plane.

On this point, there is a deep affinity between Platonist and Abrahamic-BI conceptions of the first principle's transcendence. This affinity gives the lie to the perhaps tempting thought that BB is simply a 'more transcendent' position than BI: the traditions emphatically agree that the Good or God cannot be 'in the box' of being.

The major exception to this rule in our period is, curiously enough, Aristotle – the thinker at the head of the whole BI tradition. While Aristotle's First Mover is the cause of *motion*, it is apparently not the cause of *existence* and, therefore, seems not to be ontologically transcendent in the way that Platonists and Abrahamic theologians require. Most pagan and Abrahamic thinkers in the BI tradition read (or misread) Aristotle as an ally on this issue,[147] and there is only occasional and usually oblique recognition of the problem, such as Avicenna's criticisms of those who seek 'only the principle of motion' instead of 'the principle and giver of existence' (*Meta.* VI.1).[148] From our vantage today, though, Aristotle's divergent view seems clear enough. As Richard Taylor observes: 'Aristotle seems not to have given serious consideration to being outside of or beyond what Aquinas would call *ens commune* or *esse commune*' (1998, 219). Aristotle's God seems to be an *ousia* among *ousiai*, the highest and first being among beings (*proton ton onton* – *Metaphysics* 1073a) but not the cause of beings in the Platonist sense[149] or Creator of creatures in the

---

[146] Trans. (Anselm 2007).

[147] For example, Aquinas rejects Platonist separate ideas but endorses a first principle, understood in transcendent Platonist fashion as 'essentially being and essentially good, which we call God ... and Aristotle agrees with this' (ST I.6.4 *resp.*). For the reception of Aristotle's first mover in Latin and Arabic traditions, see Alwishah and Hayes (2015) and Galluzzo and Amerini (2013).

[148] Before Avicenna, Proclus objected that Aristotle's prime mover fails to supply the 'power of existence' that the cosmos clearly possesses (Proclus, *In Tim.* II.268, trans. (2008)). On the other hand, Ammonius (175–242) and a tradition after him reads Aristotle's prime mover as causing motion *and* being, and a fascinating history of contested interpretation follows in his wake, especially in the Arabic tradition through to Maimonides and Averroes – see Twetten (2015).

[149] Cf. Eric Perl (2014, 156–7): 'Aquinas, like Plotinus, is pointing beyond Aristotle's question, "What is being?" (*Meta.* Z.1) to which essence, intelligible in virtue of form or whatness,

Abrahamic sense.[150] It is reasonable, then, to view Aristotle as an 'in the box' thinker[151] (we would meet many more if we carried our inquiry into modernity).

If, like BB thinkers, the BI tradition denies that God can be 'in the box' of beings, how should we map the BI position onto our box of being? This question presses the thought experiment to the limits of its usefulness. Probably the least false answer is to say that, for the BI tradition, God *is* the box, so long as the absolute ontological difference between uncreated 'box' and created 'contents' is somehow still retained. The meaning of 'being' attributed to the box in this case will likely differ from the meaning that is usually in play in the BB tradition, as we will see in the following.

God as Intellect, Agent, Creator, and Person

In the Neoplatonist tradition, the first principle is usually understood as 'above intellect'. For Plotinus, the One is above intellect because intellection, like being, entails plurality: even if Intellect thinks self-reflexively, so that it is 'both thinking and object of thinking', still it 'will be double, and not simple, nor will it be the One' and thus 'the One is primary, while Intellect, Forms and Being are not primary' (*Enn.* VI.9.2). Excepting Porphyry, the Neoplatonists follow Plotinus on this point, typically positioning *Nous* as a second hypostasis under the One.

---

provides a sufficient answer, to the further question, "Why are there beings, rather than nothing?"'.

[150] Cf. Avicenna (*Meta.* VIII.3.6): 'the meaning of a thing's being created ... [is] attaining existence from another'.

[151] In a careful critique of my view here, an anonymous referee argues that, while Aristotle does not endorse a BB position in the sense of Plotinus or even Aquinas, it is false that the First Mover is a being-among-beings, and, therefore, it is wrong to say that Aristotle is an 'in the box' thinker. For Aristotle, being is said in many ways, and the special sense of being (*ousia*) attributed to the First Mover distinguishes it from all other beings – as my referee observes, 'only the Unmoved Mover is being itself in the full, focal, and primary sense'. This sets the First Mover apart as transcendent in a stronger sense than merely a 'higher being among beings': 'hence the Unmoved Mover as being itself, and other things as beings in a lesser, derivative imitative sense, cannot be put together in the same box'. I do not dispute the claim that Aristotle's God is unique and even ontologically unique. The First Mover is not *just another* substance among substances; it is the unique and primary *ousia*. Nevertheless, if we take the contents-of-the-box to refer to Aquinas' *esse commune* (in the spirit of Richard Taylor's remark), then I think my judgement holds. The Aristotelian First Mover is surely different from other substances, but is it sufficiently different to transcend the community of substances to the satisfaction of Abrahamic BI (let alone BB) thinkers? In my view, the First Mover remains 'in the box' because it fails to stand outside the community of *ousia* as its cause, in the sense of 'cause of being' that the Platonists and Abrahamic traditions seek with their One and Creator. Of course, being is said in many ways, and the box metaphor can be worked in many ways, and it may be an injustice to Aristotle to measure him by Platonist/Thomistic lights like this. Nonetheless, I think this is the most illuminating way to consider Aristotle's First Mover in relation to the BI tradition that follows him. I remain grateful to my referee for their careful attention on this point.

BI thinkers, on the other hand, tend to identify the first principle with intellectuality. Several sources inform this tendency. One is Aristotle. The Aristotelian First Mover is characterised by self-reflexive thought – 'its thinking is a thinking on thinking' – and this is its actuality (*Meta.* 1075a, 1072a). Another is the Platonist construal of forms as ideas located in, or identical with, God's mind (Dillon 2019). This seems to begin in the Old Academy with Xenocrates and continues through Middle Platonist thinkers including Philo and Alcinous. If some Middle Platonists are right to interpret the 'likely story' of the *Timaeus* as a myth, so that the demiurge consulting the forms is a metaphor for the divine mind reflecting on its own ideas, then this framework may already be present in Plato as well (Gerson 2006; Perl 1998). This integration of Platonist forms with an intellectual first principle is appropriated in the theologies of many later Abrahamic thinkers, including leading patristic and medieval figures – Origen, Augustine, Aquinas, etc. (McIntosh 2021). In addition to these Aristotelian and Platonist influences, Abrahamic thinkers of course also look to biblical descriptions of God as an intellectual agent (Wisdom, Word, etc.).

Given the traditional Parmenidean being–thinking link, this BI preference for an intellectual first principle makes sense: God is *esse*, so God is also *intellegere*. Indeed, we might think of a BI position, which seems to accommodate God's intellectuality more easily than the 'beyond intellect' alternative of the BB tradition, as the more natural fit for Abrahamic monotheism.[152] We might even extend the point to include other personal characteristics in addition to intellectuality, such as agency, will, love, and creativity (in the sense of 'creator'). One might then argue that, because the first principle of monotheism cannot be a mere principle but must be a person possessing personal characteristics like these, it follows that a coherent account of this is only possible in a BI framework, not a BB one.[153]

While there may be some explanatory value in this observation – after all, most Abrahamic thinkers do hold a BI view that includes divine intellect – I think the exceptions are too many to make it a reliable rule. For instance, some BI sources construe intellect as a secondary or created principle beneath the divine pure being – for example, al-Kindi, Arabic *De causis*, Ibn Gabirol, and

---

[152] Cf. Aquinas (*In De causis* prop. 13): 'But because, according to the opinion of Aristotle (which in this agrees more [than Proclus] with Catholic doctrine), we do not maintain that there are many forms above intellects but only one, which is the first cause, we must say that, just as the first cause is being itself, so is it life itself and first intellect itself'.

[153] Cf. Rudi te Velde (2020, 130–1):

'[for Aquinas] "Being" must be the primary name of the divine cause. The reason of this is that the supreme Good of Plato must be more than an ideal principle; it must be an Aristotelian *agens*, a real principle with an effective power . . . only as identical with being can the absolute good be identified with God in the sense of an effective principle which grants being to creatures'.

the Anonymous Commentator. On the other hand, BB sources often attribute personal characteristics to their first principle. Plotinus has a detailed account of the One's will, desire, and love (*Enn.* VI.8); all Neoplatonists use *theos* talk for the One; BB Christians such as Dionysius, John Damascene, and Eriugena speak freely of God's intellect and wisdom in a 'beyond being' context, not least with respect to the Trinitarian Word. On the related issue of first principle as Creator, the familiar contrast of Greek/Platonist emanation versus Abrahamic creation is not as straightforward in the ancient and medieval period as is often assumed (Taylor 2012). Also, we should not press the claim about Abrahamic divine personality too far – few Abrahamic thinkers in our period would be attracted to what is sometimes today called 'theistic personalism', in contrast to 'classical theism' (Davies and Ruse 2021).

Revising the Meaning of 'Being'

I have suggested that BB and BI agree the first principle is not 'a being' among beings and that it therefore cannot be located 'in the box' of being. If the traditions agree on this core issue, then why do we still confront the contradict-ory language of 'beyond being' versus 'being itself'? One possible answer to this question is that BI thinkers have *revised* the meaning of 'being' so that it can accommodate the characteristics that the BB tradition attaches to the Good.

One important BI revision is the idea of infinite being (Sweeney 1992; Undusk 2009, 2012). This contrasts with the typical Greek view of being as finite, which we noted in our BB discussion. We have seen some likely beginnings of this idea in the Anonymous Commentator's undetermined *einai* and Victorinus' *esse infinitum* and *interminatum* (*Ad. Arium* IV.19). Despite the influence of Victorinus, Augustine only rarely deploys the idea explicitly – for example, God is 'a certain substance [*substantiam*] that is living, eternal, omnipotent, infinite [*infinitam*]' (*In Jo. Ev.* I.1.8).[154] In the Greek East, we earlier noted Gregory of Nyssa's novel account of infinite being. Other leading Greek and Latin Christian sources, such as Hilary of Poitiers (310–367), Dionysius, Eriugena, Peter Lombard (1096–1160), and Hugh of St Victor (1096–1141), speak of infinity of the divine nature, power, or eternity but do not affirm it specifically of divine being. After 1250, versions of infinite being became commonplace in the Latin West – for example, Albert, Henry of Ghent (1217–1293), Aquinas, Bonaventure, and many more – with Richard Fishacre (1200–1248) possibly serving as the primary innovating figure (Sweeney 1992, 319–470). These sophisticated scholastic renditions of infinite being may have been encouraged by a new integration of Aristotelian theories of matter and potency in accounting for how beings are 'determined', in addition to

---

[154] Trans. (Rettig 1988).

the inherited Platonist notion that form is the 'determining' principle. In this context, God's being is infinite in the sense that it is not determined or restricted in any way by potency. Whatever the reasons for its emergence, the notion of infinite being offers BI thinkers a way of attributing *einai* or *esse* to the first principle while still accommodating the BB demand for transcendence beyond (finite) beings.

Another BI revision to the meaning of 'being' develops with the doctrine of transcendentals in the medieval Latin tradition (Aertsen 2012). As being is configured to be identical with Good, so it is configured to be identical also with unity, truth, beauty, thing (*res*), and something (*aliquid*) – the details vary in different thinkers – and this supports the attribution of being to God, who medieval thinkers agree possesses all perfections.

Such revisions mean that, more often than not, when BI thinkers attribute 'being' to the first principle, they attribute something other than the 'being' which BB thinkers deny of it.[155]

From Above versus from Below

There is a basic conceptual difficulty in thinking about transcendence, which has been present under the surface in much of the material we have considered in this study. How can a first principle be (a) absolutely transcendent above all beings, yet also (b) cause of those beings and source of their characteristics and excellences? This looks like a dilemma. If the First has a causal relationship to the plurality of beings and their characteristics, then it seems impossible for it to be strictly simple, transcendent, and independent of them. As many interpreters have noticed, this transcendence versus causality problem is intrinsic to Platonist thinking about the first principle (Greig 2020, 25; Riel 2016, 76). (Indeed, it seems to be reflected in most or all of the world's philosophical/ religious traditions that contend with transcendence.)[156]

---

[155] Cf. Norris Clarke (1959, 80): 'the apparently unbridgeable gap between Plotinian infinite nonbeing and Christian infinite being is largely an artificial one, created by playing on the two terms as though they meant the same in both climates of thought … the "nonbeing" of [Plotinus's] One … [signifies] the most supremely real and positively perfect of all realities, precisely because it is above all particular limited beings as their ultimate source'.

[156] Ahbel-Rappe (Damascius 2009, 161) writes:

'one of Neoplatonism's central dilemmas [is] caused by the tensions between a One that is utterly transcendent vs. the One conceived as first principle, source of all subsequent stages of reality. The significance of this discussion cannot be underestimated, as the various ways of conceiving the first principle, in terms of an ultimately negative theology or in terms of an attributive (or kataphatic) theology, have informed theological inquiry in Christian, Muslim, and Jewish traditions, largely echoing Neoplatonist formulations … it is at the heart of theological inquiries almost universally'.

The figures we have considered are drawn to both horns of the dilemma. Maximus speaks for many in both BB and BI traditions when he notes the appeal of *being* talk for 'affirming the being of God as cause of beings' and the equal appeal of *non-being* talk for 'completely denying in him the being which all beings have, based on his preeminence as cause' (*Mystagogia* 664AC). The BI tradition, encouraged in some cases by Abrahamic commitments, tends to emphasise the causality of the First, by emphasising that *ipsum esse* pre-contains all perfections and typically recognising a legitimate analogical ascription of perfections to the first cause and its effects. The BB tradition tends to emphasise the transcendence of the First, deploying the *epekeina* to underscore the absolute distinction between finite being and the First.[157] But I think that we can see these BB and BI emphases as two perspectives on the same difficulty, one 'from above' and one 'from below'.[158] Seen this way, the perspectives can plausibly be reconciled, a possibility we will explore further in the next section.

3 Reconciling the Traditions?

Having completed our historical sketches of the BB and BI traditions, I now want to consider whether these traditions are in fact as opposed as they appear. To say that the first principle is 'beyond being' seems incompatible with, and maybe even a precise antithesis of, the claim that the first principle is 'being itself'. Is this true?

Irreconcilable Traditions

In recent times, a set of influential Western Catholic and Eastern Orthodox scholars have argued that it is indeed true. On the Eastern side, Christos Yannaras sees 'an insurmountable contrast on the level of ontology as well as epistemology' between the Western 'apophaticism of divine *being*' and the 'Christian thought of the Greek East' (2005, 23–30). 'The absolutizing of the existential fact' in Western theological understandings of God as pure act 'continues to limit the ontological problem to the field of abstract definitions' and indeed contributes to a 'difference between Byzantium and the West [which] is a difference between two comprehensive epistemological-ethical views of the world, humanity and God' (2007, 22, 220). Yannaras' argument develops Vladimir Lossky's celebration of the Eastern BB way of thinking in opposition to Western scholastic approaches (1957).

---

[157] Still, even Plotinus (*Enn.* V.3.15), the arch-BB thinker, recognises the causal requirement and describes the One as 'the productive power of all things [*dunamis pantos*]'.

[158] Wayne Hankey (1980, 145): 'both sides [i.e. BB and BI Platonists] are endeavouring to think how the first can both be transcendent and yet all things be in and derive from it as their source–though perhaps they are looking at this problem from its opposite ends'.

Some twentieth-century Thomists, pre-eminently Étienne Gilson, see a similar contradiction between the BB and BI traditions but defend the other side of the divide. 'No Christian philosophy can posit anything above Being', Gilson argues (1952, 30), and he condemns Victorinus, Dionysius, Eriugena, and Eckhart for doing so (1952, 1–40; 2002, 137–74). To affirm a 'beyond being' is 'absolutely inconsistent with the mental universe of Christian thinkers … one cannot think, at one and the same time, as a Neoplatonist and as a Christian' (1952, 31). For Gilson, the BI position is a straightforward antithesis of the BB approach: in Aquinas' theory of *esse*, 'the entire doctrine of [Pseudo-Dionysius] … is here inverted' (1994, 140).

Such overtly antagonistic presentations of BB versus BI are surprisingly rare in the historical sources, perhaps due to a common (though not universal) conviction in our period that the great authorities of the past agree, if only their texts are rightly interpreted and harmonised (Adamson 2022; Karamanolis 2006). One illuminating instance of explicit antagonism, however, is Proclus' critique of those who say that the Good has a peculiar sort of existence above being (*In Rem* XI.282).[159] 'What prevents the Good, they say, from both being existent [*ousia*] and superessential [*huperousia*]?'[160] Proclus replies that it is 'not true that the Good has existence in a different sense of existence [*ousia*]', and explains:

> This is because there is only one signification of being belonging to all of the intelligibles, which we say both 'is' [*einai*] and 'genuinely is' [*ontos einai*]. But since the Good is established above these things, what kind of existence [*ousia*] is left for it, in accordance with which it is an existence [*ousia*] and not solely superessential [*huperousion*]? All existence [*ousia*] is of necessity being [*on*], but Socrates said that the Good was not beyond existence [*ousias*] alone but also beyond being [*einai*]. Therefore one ought not to say that the Good exists [*einai*], since it is beyond existing [*epekeina tou einai estin*]. (*In Rem* XI.282)

Proclus argues here that there is no linguistic or metaphysical likeness between the ontological standing of beings and the standing of the One. He puts his finger on the decisive issue here, I think – *what kind of being is left for the first principle, if it is beyond all beings?* If the answer to this question is, as Proclus suggests, 'none', then BB and BI do indeed appear to be fundamentally opposed ways of thinking.

---

[159] Trans. (Proclus 2018).
[160] It is not clear who Proclus has in view here – it may be Neoplatonists such as Porphyry or Amelius or maybe earlier Middle Platonists.

Reconcilable Traditions

If, on the other hand, the Anonymous Commentator could be right that 'being is double' in some sense, then there may be another kind of being available for the First, and it may be possible to harmonise BB and BI positions. To explore this possibility, let us consider a passage from Aquinas' commentary on Proposition 6 of the *Liber de causis*. This text offers, I think, a model instance of reconciling the core claims of the BB and BI traditions. The historical–textual background of Aquinas' *De causis* commentary makes it especially fitting for this task of cross-tradition synthesis. Aquinas' commentary (1272 Paris) expounds a Latin translation by Gerard of Cremona (twelfth-century Toledo) of an Arabic adaptation, likely penned by a Syriac Christian in the circle of Muslim philosopher al-Kindi (ninth-century Bagdhad) of metaphysical writings by Proclus the pagan Neoplatonist (fifth-century Egypt-Greece), which are inspired by Greek philosophy's great master, Plato (fifth-century BCE Athens). This long, rich inheritance in Aquinas' *De causis* commentary well reflects the intellectual paths that we have been tracing through this study, which run through a vast breadth of Western histories, languages, and geographies.

In our passage, Aquinas addresses the central question of our study: in what sense is the first principle beyond being, or being itself? He begins by citing the Platonist BB position:

> [T]he first cause is above being [*supra ens*] … According to the Platonists, however, the first cause is above being [*supra ens*] inasmuch as the essence of goodness and unity, which is the first cause, also surpasses [*excedit*] separated being itself [*ipsum ens*], as was said above. But, according to the truth of the matter, the first cause is above being [*supra ens*] inasmuch as it is itself infinite 'to be' [*ipsum esse infinitum*]. 'Being', [*ens*] however, is called that which finitely participates 'to be', [*esse*] and it is this which is proportioned to our intellect, whose object is some 'that which is' [*quod quid est*], as it is said in Book 3 of *On the Soul*. Hence our intellect can grasp only that which has a quiddity participating 'to be' [*esse*]. But the quiddity of God is 'to be' itself [*ipsum esse*]. Thus it is above the intellect … and it is evident that the first cause transcends description. (*In De causis* prop. 6)

Aquinas here accepts the core BB claim that the first principle is above being (*supra ens*) and agrees that it is rightly characterised as goodness and unity. He even cites the Platonist view that the Good or One 'surpasses' – no doubt in the sense of Platonic *epekeina* – not just beings but separated being itself (*ipsum esse*), and embraces the position for his own, even if he explicates it in a particular way in the next sentence. This sympathetic treatment of BB transcendence is in keeping with Aquinas' view, as discussed earlier, that God is located outside *esse commune* and outside the order of beings. It is in keeping also with his view articulated elsewhere that, despite his criticisms of the *Platonici* on issues such as separated ideas, 'as regards what [the Platonists] said about the first principle of things, their opinion is most true and harmonizes with the Christian faith' (*In Div. Nom.* proem 2).[161] Thus, Aquinas, like many before him,[162] sees a natural fit between Platonist talk about a Good beyond being and Abrahamic talk – including BI talk – about God.

In addition to recognising an intellectual comrade in Plato, Aquinas also indicates in this passage how BI and BB frameworks can be integrated. He distinguishes between two senses of being: first, God's infinite *esse* which is identical with his quiddity, and second, the finite *ens* of creatures, which exists only by participating in *esse*. Aquinas explains that while our minds can grasp the quiddities of finite *entia*, the divine *esse* is its own quiddity, and so it transcends our capacities of thought and language. These two modes of *esse* are related metaphysically by participation and linguistically/epistemologically (though Aquinas does not spell this out here) through analogy. With this distinction in hand, Aquinas can argue that the BB position (*supra ens*) is secured precisely through the first principle's peculiar ontological standing: God is beyond *ens* inasmuch as he is *ipsum esse infinitum*. God is located beyond being by his infinity of being. This represents, I think, a plausible way of reconciling the two traditions we have outlined in this study.[163]

This passage also stands as a Thomistic reply to Proclus' objection to BI positions. Proclus asks: 'since the Good is established above these things, what kind of existence is left for it?' For Aquinas, the other 'kind of existence' available for the Good is *esse divinum*. 'God's being [*esse divinum*], which is his essence, is not common being [*esse commune*], but being [*esse*] distinct from all other being, so that by his very being [*esse*], God is distinct from every other being' (*De pot.* 7.2 ad 4).

Aquinas' exposition of the *Liber de causis* invites us to say – contra Gilson, Yannaras, and company – that we can in fact reconcile BB and BI.[164] This compatibilist view is shared by a good number of contemporary interpreters of the BB and BI traditions. William Franke, for instance, judges that the apparent BB–BI contradiction is in reality 'a matter of sensibility and outlook and ultimately

---

[161] Cf. *ST* I.6.4 *resp.* For this reason, he also endorses Dionysian descriptions of God as super-good (*superbonum*) and super-substance (*supersubstantiam*) (*In Div. nom.* proem).

[162] For example, Albert praises 'the wisdom of Plato' regarding the first principle (*Summa de mirabili scientia dei* 2, q. 3, m. 3, a. 2) (Vargas 2013), and Augustine (*Civ. dei* 8.11) sees his own BI view as previously articulated 'with the greatest possible care by Plato'.

[163] Another passage that might be used for this purpose is Maximus' discussion of God's *huparxin* beyond *ousia* at *Mystagogia* 664 AC.

[164] Cf. Edward Booth (1983, 207n5): '[Gilson has a] too limited conception of "Thomas, the Aristotelian," to whom Platonism is the evident enemy. But such a misunderstanding is an unconscious witness to Thomas' complete success in so combining Aristotelian with Platonist, Cryptoproclean ideas that neither is disturbed'.

of modes of relationship' (2007, 15). John Rist argues that Augustine's BI position 'clarifies and advances the intent while often discarding the vocabulary of Neoplatonism' (2007, 86). Eric Perl suggests that the 'all too common' opposition of Aquinas' God with Plotinus' One is based on 'nothing more than a difference of terminology, and in large part an accident of translation' (2011a, 185). Reflecting on the Jewish tradition, Sarah Pessin argues that Gabirol's God of pure being can be 'consistently and meaningfully be described in Plotinus' own terms as a One "above being"' (2003, 100). In a passage worth quoting at length, David Bentley Hart argues that opposing 'beyond being' and 'being itself' is 'simply a false opposition, inasmuch as the word "being" is certainly not univocal between the two usages':

> When the Greek fathers spoke of God as Being – as, that is, *to ontos on* (etc.) – or when Latin theologians, patristic or mediaeval, spoke of God as *ens, actus essendi subsistens*, or *esse* (etc.), they were speaking of God as the transcendent source and end of all things, whose being is not merely the opposite of nonbeing, and in whom there is no unrealised potential, deficiency, or change. But it is precisely in this sense that God is also (to use the venerable Platonic phrase) *epekeina tēs ousias:* 'superessential', 'supersubstantial', 'beyond being'. That is, he wholly transcends 'beings', and discrete 'substances', and the 'totality of substances', and the created being in which all beings share; and no concept we possess of beings or of being makes it possible for us to comprehend him.
>   . . . In either case, there is no *conceptum univocum entis* to span the divide between divine and created being, and thus the true distinction to be drawn is not one between two incompatible ways of naming God, peculiar respectively to West and East, but between two forms of the same name, corresponding to two distinct moments within what I would be content to call the 'analogy of being' (2008, 196–8).

This proposed BB–BI compatibility encourages us to see the BB and BI traditions as pursuing a common intellectual project of inquiry into transcendence. The thinkers we have considered use a wide set of vocabularies to indicate a first principle that is *epekeina, huper, super, ultra,* and *beyond* beings. The decision whether to subsequently attribute a special sense of 'being' to the first principle in BI fashion is, in a sense, internal to this primary project of distinguishing the origin of being from the beings to which it gives existence – that is, of clarifying why the origin of being cannot be 'in the box'. Seen this way, the differing languages of BB and BI are 'in house' differences – they represent alternative but compatible ways of articulating transcendence.[165] BB and BI are therefore, I suggest, different ways of saying the same thing.

---

[165] However, might we not object, as a perceptive anonymous referee of this manuscript suggests, that there are major BI thinkers, especially Augustine, who ultimately do not share the 'not in the box' conviction that is essential to BB? Answering this satisfactorily would require a

4 God and Being Today

To conclude this Element, I will suggest a couple of ways that our findings can contribute to current discussions in philosophy of religion.

First, in analytic philosophy of religion, some recent treatments of apophatic theological language engage explicitly with the BB and BI traditions. In particular, Michael Rea develops a view that welcomes an apophatic and analogical dimension in perfection attributions such as goodness, love, and justice, but not being (2018, 42–62; 2020). Despite sympathies with the BB and BI traditions, he argues that they both falter because a theologically satisfactory account of divine existence requires that 'being' is attributed to God not metaphorically or even analogically but literally and univocally. Existence talk must be literal/ univocal because 'unlike other predicates (like "is good" or "is loving") that are ripe for apophatic treatment, there is no theological reason for thinking that existence-words express merely "creaturely" modes of being' (2020, 135). Indeed, he argues that those who distinguish between divine and creaturely modes of being are not rightly called 'theists' because they fail to attribute existence in the usual sense to God. Rea's judgement likely rules out every historical figure we have considered in this study. (If Avicenna, Maimonides, and Aquinas cannot manage to be theists, what hope for the rest of us!)

Our study's findings can intervene here. The shared claim of the BB and BI traditions is that, if God is truly to be the cause of creatures, he simply cannot be

---

case-by-case analysis at a level of detail not possible here. But let us glance at Augustine as an exemplary instance. My referee argues that God for Augustine is pure intelligible being, whereas, for Plotinus and Aquinas, God transcends intelligible being as its principle, and so Augustine falls short of BB transcendence. (Cf. Eric Perl (2011b, 770): 'The difference between Dionysius' and Augustine's Christian versions of Platonism is instructive ... Augustine's God is fundamentally pure intellect, pure form, pure being, and the Platonic idea of the first principle as beyond all these is to a large extent lost'.) I agree that reconciling BI to BB is a tougher task in Augustine than in Aquinas, since Aquinas' distinction of creaturely and divine *esse*, with the latter explicitly lying *supra ens*, is not anticipated straightforwardly in his predecessor (though the possibility noted earlier of Victorinus' act-*einai-esse* transmitting to Augustine would make this more likely). Nevertheless, I think there is an alternative framework in Augustine for making the same point, namely the contrast of God's perfect existence with creatures' 'non-existence' – a created thing 'slips away, flows off, and holds onto nothing actual, that is, to speak Latin, it does not exist [*non esse*]' (*Epist.* 2, trans. (Augustine 2001)). This view aligns with Rist (2007). We might worry that Augustine has failed to think past a simple Platonist sensible/ intelligible distinction here; but I think this underappreciates the intervention of his Creator/ creature commitments, which cut across the inherited Greek distinction. This is why Marion can speak of an Augustinian 'equivocity of being', a phrase that I noted earlier with some reservations but which makes the relevant point here: Augustine can be read as affirming the BB principle from within a different conceptual framework and this is Augustine's version of the BI commitment to 'not a being among beings', discussed in the 'Logic of BI' section earlier. In this vein, the essays by Hart, Marion, and Bradshaw in Demacopoulos and Papanikolaou (2008) can be read together as an illuminating debate about how to position Augustine with respect to BB and BI thinking.

another being among these beings. This conviction requires that we distinguish a creaturely mode of existence from God's mode of existence and thus develop some sort of 'double being' structure (to use the Anonymous Commentator's phrase). In the BB and BI traditions, versions of this structure are articulated using the plethora of terminologies for created beings we have encountered in this study: contingent being, finite being, common being, participated being, etc. This basic logic of classical theism can, I think, supply Rea with his missing 'theological reason' for distinguishing divine and creaturely ontology. Perhaps, it could also motivate a conscientious analytic reception of historic BB and/or BI theories,[166] in the way that a recent analytic work has examined, for example, creedal Christological claims (Pawl 2016).

Turning to Continental philosophy of religion, the findings of study are relevant to debates about Heidegger's critique of ontotheology. Ontotheology refers to conceptual systems that coordinate God and beings as mutually explanatory entities. Or, as my preferred working definition goes: 'ontotheology, that is, God being part and parcel of the general being of the world'.[167] Heidegger worries that ontotheology occludes philosophical inquiry by giving pat answers to profound questions about Being and that it produces a philosopher's God that is useless for true religion: 'man can neither fall to his knees in awe nor can he play music and dance before this god' (Heidegger 1969, 72).[168]

More or less endorsing Heidegger's critique, a set of recent Continental philosophers have responded by seeking a non-ontotheological approach to theology and religion (Gschwandtner 2013). Working in the wake of Levinas' retrieval of Plato for his 'otherwise than being' (Levinas 1991) and energised by Derrida's engagement with negative theology (Derrida 1992), some of these scholars retrieve BB historical figures for this purpose, most often Pseudo-Dionysius (Marion 1995; Yannaras 2005) but also Eriugena (Moran 2004, 99–102), Eckhart (Moore 2018; Rubenstein 2003), and others. Crudely put, the appeal of the BB tradition here is that, if God is not captured by being, then he is not captured by ontotheology. Thus, with a BB God, religion and theology can renew itself for a post-Heideggerian future.

---

[166] Cf. Sarah Coakley's (2013, 6) hope, expressed in the early days of analytic theology, that going forward 'the analytic wing is willing to admit the *sui generis* ontological status of the divine'. Work in this direction includes Jacobs (2015).

[167] Marion (2005, 146). Heidegger's own definition is articulated in Heidegger (1969).

[168] Despite his critique of ontotheology, Heidegger (1998, 181) remains curiously blind to the Platonist thought of a BB principle exceeding creaturely ontology. He sees Plato as a founder of ontotheology and Plato's Good as merely 'the being-est of beings', and he pays hardly any attention to the Neoplatonists. Yet, equally curiously, at points, Heidegger (2002) seems to positively echo BB thinking, as in his notion of *Ereignis* that 'gives' being. I am grateful to an anonymous referee and to my doctoral student, Emile Alexandrov, for suggestions on this point.

Our major proposal in this study, namely that the BB and BI traditions are complementary, can widen this Continental project of 'overcoming' ontotheology. If the step beyond being can indeed escape ontotheology, then perhaps thinkers in the BI tradition, at least as we have traced it up to Aquinas, can do the same, with the step *supra ens* made now by way of *ipsum esse* and with the BI *analogia* doing the same work as the BB *epekeina*. Jean-Luc Marion's later work on Aquinas, Anselm, and Augustine, and Emmanuel Falque's work on Bonaventure are two exemplars here (Falque 2018; Marion 1992, 2003, 2012). Such retrievals of BI thinkers can also correspond with the 'return of metaphysics' in recent post-postmodern Continental philosophy (Sparrow 2014). If a reconsideration of the BI tradition in this way is plausible, then Heidegger's historical diagnosis of ontotheology will need a reconsideration as well (Hankey 2004). Heidegger locates the beginning of ontotheology at the Presocratic–Socratic transition, but it may be the case that ontotheology in a pernicious sense properly begins much later, perhaps with Scotus, Henry of Ghent (1293–1217), or Francisco Suárez (1548–1617), as a number of intellectual historians have proposed (Boulnois 2016; Miner 2001).[169]

Conclusion

In the remark cited as an epigraph to this Element, Origen laments that 'there is much to say which is hard to perceive about being' and points to the particular difficulty of working out 'whether God transcends being ... or whether He is Himself being' (*Contra Celsum* VI.64). Origen is not alone in perceiving the difficulty of this task. Aristotle says that 'the question which is hardest of all and most perplexing' is 'whether unity and being, as the Pythagoreans and Plato said, are not attributes of something else but are the substance of existing things' (*Meta.* 996a). Indeed, this is 'the hardest inquiry of all, and the one most necessary for knowledge of the truth' (*Meta.* 1001a). Aristotle and Origen ask versions of the same hard question – is there a single principle of existence, and how is it related to the being of existing things? This study has not attempted to answer this hardest of questions directly, only to sketch the two major answers given to it in the premodern Western traditions. If our study does provide some reply to Origen's question – *is God beyond being or being itself?* – then it is this: the answer could be 'both'.

---

[169] Daniel Horan defends Scotus against these charges in Horan (2014). Horan is responding to the work of John Milbank and Catherine Pickstock, which brought the Scotus intellectual history debates to prominence in theology – see, for example, Milbank (2018) and Pickstock (2005).

References

Adamson, Peter. 2002a. 'Before Essence and Existence: Al-Kindi's Conception of Being'. *Journal of the History of Philosophy* 40 (3): 297–312. https://doi.org/10/b26hnt.

——— 2002b. *The Arabic Plotinus: A Philosophical Study of the Theology of Aristotle*. London: Bloomsbury.

——— 2022. *Don't Think for Yourself: Authority and Belief in Medieval Philosophy*. South Bend, IN: University of Notre Dame Press.

Addey, Crystal. 2016. *Divination and Theurgy in Neoplatonism: Oracles of the Gods*. New York: Routledge.

Aertsen, Jan. 2012. *Medieval Philosophy as Transcendental Thought: From Philip the Chancellor to Francisco Súarez*. Leiden: Brill.

Albert the Great. 1988. 'Commentary on Dionysius' Mystical Theology'. In *Albert & Thomas: Selected Writings*, edited and translated by Simon Tugwell, 131–98. New York: Paulist Press.

Al-Ghazali. 2002. *The Incoherence of the Philosophers*. Translated by Michael Marmura. Provo, UT: Brigham Young University Press.

Al-Sijistānī. 1994. *The Wellsprings of Wisdom: A Study of Abū Yaʿqūb Al-Sijistānī's Kitāb Al-Yanābīʿ*. Translated by Paul E. Walker. Salt Lake City, UT: University of Utah Press.

Altman, Alexander, and Samuel Miklos Stern, eds. 2010. *Isaac Israeli: A Neoplatonic Philosopher of the Early Tenth Century*. Chicago, IL: University of Chicago Press.

Alwishah, Ahmed, and Josh Hayes, eds. 2015. *Aristotle and the Arabic Tradition*. Cambridge: Cambridge University Press.

Anselm. 1979. *St. Anselm's Proslogion: With a Reply on Behalf of the Fool by Gaunilo and the Author's Reply to Gaunilo*. Translated by Maxwell John Charlesworth. South Bend, IN: University of Notre Dame Press.

——— 2007. *Anselm: Basic Writings*. Translated by Thomas Williams. Indianapolis, IN: Hackett.

Aquinas, Thomas. 1920. *The Summa Theologica*. Translated by The Fathers of the English Dominican Province. 3 vols. London: Burns, Oates, and Washbourne.

——— 1949. *On Spiritual Creatures*. Edited by Mary C. Fitzpatrick and John J. Wellmuth. Milwaukee, WI: Marquette University Press.

——— 1952. *On the Power of God*. Translated by The English Dominican Fathers. Westminster, MA: Newman Press.

1955. *On the Truth of the Catholic Faith: Summa Contra Gentiles*. Translated by James F. Anderson, Vernon J. Bourke, Anton Pegis, and Charles J. O'Neil. 4 vols. New York: Hanover House.

1962. *Aristotle: On Interpretation, Commentary by St. Thomas and Cajetan*. Translated by Jean T. Oesterle. Milwaukee, WI: Marquette University Press.

1968. *On Being and Essence*. Translated by Armand Maurer. Toronto: Pontifical Institute of Mediaeval Studies.

1996. *Commentary on the Book of Causes*. Translated by Vincent A. Guagliardo, Charles R. Hess, and Richard C. Taylor. Washington, DC: Catholic University of America Press.

1997. *Thomas Aquinas's Earliest Treatment of the Divine Essence (Sent. I.8)*. Translated by Edward M. Macierowski. Binghamtom, NY: Binghamton University.

2022. *An Exposition of the Divine Names, the Book of Blessed Dionysius*. Translated by Michael Augros. Merrimack, NH: Thomas More College Press.

Aristotle. 1984a. 'Metaphysics'. In *Complete Works of Aristotle, Vol. 1*, edited by Jonathan Barnes, translated by William David Ross, 1552–1728. Princeton, NJ: Princeton University Press.

1984b. 'Physics'. In *Complete Works of Aristotle, Vol. 1*, edited by Jonathan Barnes, translated by Robert Purves Hardie and R. K. Gaye. page range = 315–446 Princeton, NJ: Princeton University Press.

Augustine. 1990. *Sermons on the Old Testament (1–19)*. Translated by Edmund Hill. New York: New City Press.

1991. *Confessions*. Translated by Henry Chadwick. Oxford: Oxford University Press.

2001. *Letters 1–99*. Translated by Roland Teske. New York: New City Press.

2002. *The Trinity*. Translated by Stephen McKenna. The Fathers of the Church 45. Washington, DC: Catholic University of America Press.

2004. *Expositions of the Psalms, 121–150*. Translated by Maria Boulding. Hyde Park, NY: New City Press.

2010. *The Catholic and Manichaean Ways of Life*. Translated by Donald A. Gallagher and Idella J. Gallagher. Washington, DC: Catholic University of America Press.

Averroes. 2016. *Averroes' Tahafut Al-Tahafut: The Incoherence of the Incoherence*. Translated by Simon van den Bergh. London: Gibb Memorial Trust.

Avicenna. 2005. *The Metaphysics of the Healing*. Translated by Michael E. Marmura. Provo, UT: Brigham Young University Press.

Baltes, Matthias. 1997. 'Is the Idea of the Good in Plato's Republic Beyond Being?' In *Studies in Plato and the Platonic Tradition*, edited by Mark Joyal, 3–24. London: Routledge.

Bechtle, Gerald. 1999. *The Anonymous Commentary on Plato's 'Parmenides'*. Bern: Verlag P. Haupt.

Berthold, George C., trans. 1985. 'The Church's Mystagogy'. In *Selected Writings*, edited by Maximus the Confessor, 181–226. New York: Paulist Press.

Bertolacci, Amos. 2020. 'God's Existence and Essence: The Liber de Causis and School Discussions in the Metaphysics of Avicenna'. In *Reading Proclus and the Book of Causes, Volume 2: Translations and Acculturations*, edited by Dragos Calma, 251–80. Leiden: Brill.

Boethius. 1968. *The Theological Tractates and the Consolation of Philosophy*. Translated by Hugh Fraser Stewart and Edward Kennard Rand. Cambridge, MA: Harvard University Press.

Bonaventure. 2002. *Itinerarium Mentis in Deum*. Translated by Zachary Hayes. New York: Franciscan Institute.

Booth, Edward. 1983. *Aristotelian Aporetic Ontology in Islamic and Christian Thinkers*. Cambridge: Cambridge University Press.

Boulnois, Olivier. 1999. *Être et représentation: Une généalogie de la métaphysique moderne à l'époque de Duns Scot (XIIIe–XIVe siècle)*. Paris: Presses Universitaires de France. https://doi.org/10.3917/puf .bouln.1999.01.

2016. 'When Does Ontotheology Begin? Aristotle, Thomas Aquinas, and Duns Scotus'. Translated by Nathan Strunk. *Arc: The Journal of the School of Religious Studies, McGill University* 44 (January): 1–30.

Boys-Stones, George. 2017. *Platonist Philosophy 80 BC to AD 250: An Introduction and Collection of Sources in Translation*. Cambridge: Cambridge University Press.

Bradshaw, David. 1999. 'Neoplatonic Origins of the Act of Being'. *The Review of Metaphysics* 3: 383–401.

2004. *Aristotle East and West: Metaphysics and the Division of Christendom*. New York: Cambridge University Press.

2008. 'Augustine the Metaphysician'. In *Orthodox Readings of Augustine*, edited by George Demacopoulos and Aristotle Papanikolaou, 227–52. Crestwood, NY: St. Vladimir's Seminary Press.

Brock, Stephen L. 2007. 'Harmonizing Plato and Aristotle on Esse: Thomas Aquinas and the De Hebdomadibus'. *Nova et Vetera* 5 (3): 465–93.

Burnyeat, Myles F. 2006. 'Platonism in the Bible: Numenius of Apamea on Exodus and Eternity'. In *The Revelation of the Name YHWH to Moses: Perspectives from Judaism, the Pagan Graeco-Roman World, and Early Christianity*, edited by Geurt Hendrik van Kooten, 139–68. Leiden: Brill.

Byers, Sarah. 2022. '"Consubstantiality" as a Philosophical-Theological Problem: Victorinus' Hylomorphic Model of God and His "Correction"

References

by Augustine'. *Scottish Journal of Theology* 75 (1): 12–22. https://doi.org/
10.1017/S0036930621000788.

Calcidius. 2016. *On Plato's Timaeus*. Translated by John Magee. Cambridge,
MA: Harvard University Press.

Carabine, Deirdre. 1992a. 'Negative Theology in the Thought of Saint
Augustine'. *Recherches de Théologie et Philosophie Médiévales* 59: 5–22.
https://doi.org/10.2143/RTPM.59.0.2016285.

1992b. *The Unknown God: Negative Theology in the Platonic Tradition:
Plato to Eriugena*. Louvain: Peeters.

2000. *John Scottus Eriugena*. Oxford: Oxford University Press.

Chase, Michael. 2020. 'Porphyry and the Theology of Aristotle'. In *Reading
Proclus and the Book of Causes, Volume 2: Translations and Acculturations*,
edited by Dragos Calma, 157–81. Leiden: Brill.

2022. 'Essence and Existence in Marius Victorinus and in Avicenna'. In
The Philosophy, Theology, and Rhetoric of Marius Victorinus, edited
by Stephen A. Cooper and Václav Němec, 457–80. Atlanta: SBL Press.

Clark, Dennis. 2017. 'The Anonymous Commentary on the Parmenides'. In
Brill's Companion to the Reception of Plato in Antiquity, edited by Harold
Tarrant, Dirk Baltzly, François Renaud, and Danielle A. Layne, 351–65.
Leiden: Brill.

Clark, Mary T. 1972. 'The Neoplatonism of Marius Victorinus'. *Studia Patristica*
108: 13–19.

2007. 'The Synthesis Tradition'. In *Divine Creation in Ancient, Medieval,
and Early Modern Thought*, edited by Willemien Otten, Walter Hannam,
and Michael Treschow, 285–94. Leiden: Brill.

2009. 'The Earliest Philosophy of The Living God'. *Proceedings of the
American Catholic Philosophical Association* 41: 87–93.

Clarke, William Norris. 1959. 'Infinity in Plotinus: A Reply'. *Gregorianum*
40 (1): 75–98.

Coakley, Sarah. 2013. 'On Why Analytic Theology Is Not a Club'. *Journal of
the American Academy of Religion* 81, 3: 601–8. https://doi.org/10.1093/
jaarel/lft040.

Cooper, Stephen. 2016. 'The Platonist Christianity of Marius Victorinus'.
Religions 7 (10): 122. https://doi.org/10/gm53d2.

Corrigan, Kevin. 1984. 'A Philosophical Precursor to the Theory of Essence
and Existence in St. Thomas Aquinas'. *The Thomist: A Speculative
Quarterly Review* 48 (2): 219–40. https://doi.org/10/gkmst4.

2011. 'The Place of the Parmenides in Plato's Thought and in the Subsequent
Tradition'. In *Plato's Parmenides and Its Heritage Vol. 1, History and*

Interpretation from the Old Academy to Later Platonism and Gnosticism, edited by John Turner and Kevin Corrigan, 23–36. Leiden: Brill.

Corrigan, Kevin, and Tuomas Rasimus, eds. 2013. *Gnosticism, Platonism and the Late Ancient World*. Leiden: Brill.

Courtine, Jean-François. 2014. 'Essence, Substance, Subsistence, Existence'. In *Dictionary of Untranslatables: A Philosophical Lexicon*, edited by Barbara Cassin, Emily Apter, Jacques Lezra, and Michael Wood, translated by Steven Rendall, Christian Hubert, Jeffrey Mehlman, Nathanael Stein, and Michael Syrotinski, 298–311. Princeton, NJ: Princeton University Press.

Cullen, Christopher M., and Franklin T. Harkins, eds. 2019. *The Discovery of Being and Thomas Aquinas*. Washington, DC: Catholic University of America Press.

Damascene, John. 1958. *St. John of Damascus: Writings*. Translated by Frederic H. Chase Jr. Washington, DC: Catholic University of America Press.

Damascius. 2009. *Problems and Solutions Concerning First Principles*. Translated by Sara Ahbel-Rappe. Oxford: Oxford University Press.

D'Ancona, Cristina. 2000. 'Avicenna and the Liber de Causis: A Contribution to the Dossier'. *Revista Española de Filosofía Medieval* 7 (October): 95–114. https://doi.org/10.21071/refime.v7i.9442.

D'Ancona, Cristina. 2011. 'Platonic and Neoplatonic Terminology for Being in Arabic Translation'. *Studia Graeco-Arabica* 1: 23–46.

D'Ancona, Cristina. 2023. 'Anniyya Faqat Again'. In *Contextualizing Premodern Philosophy: Explorations of the Greek, Hebrew, Arabic, and Latin Traditions*, edited by Katja Krause, Luis Xavier López-Farjeat, and Nicholas A. Oschman, 225–45. New York: Routledge. https://doi.org/10.4324/9781003309895.

D'Ancona, Cristina. 1995. *Recherches sur le Liber De Causis*. Paris: Vrin.

Davies, Brian. 1996. 'The Mystery of God: Aquinas and McCabe'. *New Blackfriars* 77 (906): 335–47. https://doi.org/10.1111/j.1741-2005.1996.tb01566.x.

Davies, Brian, and Michael Ruse. 2021. *Taking God Seriously: Two Different Voices*. Cambridge: Cambridge University Press.

Demacopoulos, George, and Aristotle Papanikolaou, eds. 2008. *Orthodox Readings of Augustine*. Crestwood, NY: St. Vladimir's Seminary Press.

Derrida, Jacques. 1992. 'How to Avoid Speaking: Denials'. In *Derrida and Negative Theology*, edited by Harold Coward and Toby Foshay, translated by Ken Frieden, 73–142. Albany, NY: State University of New York Press.

Desjardins, Rosemary. 2003. *Plato and the Good: Illuminating the Darkling Vision*. Leiden: Brill.

Dillon, John. 2003. *The Heirs of Plato: A Study of the Old Academy (347–274 BC)*. Oxford: Oxford University Press.

2007. 'Numenius: Some Ontological Questions'. *Bulletin of the Institute of Classical Studies.* Supplement 94: 397–402. https://doi.org/10.1111/j.2041-5370.2007.tb02437.x.

2019. 'The Ideas as Thoughts of God'. In *The Roots of Platonism: The Origins and Chief Features of a Philosophical Tradition*, 35–49. Cambridge: Cambridge University Press. https://doi.org/10.1017/9781108584906.005.

Drozdek, Adam. 2016. *Greek Philosophers as Theologians: The Divine Arche.* London: Routledge.

Endress, Gerhard. 1997. 'The Circle of Al-Kindi: Early Arabic Translations from the Greek and the Rise of Islamic Philosophy'. In *The Ancient Tradition in Christian and Islamic Hellenism, Studies on the Transmission of Greek Philosophy and Sciences*, edited by Gerhard Endress and Remke Kruk, 43–76. Leiden: CNWS.

Falque, Emmanuel. 2018. *Saint Bonaventure and the Entrance of God Into Theology.* Translated by Brian Lapsa, Sarah Horton, and William C. Hackett. New York: Franciscan Institute.

Ferber, Rafael, and Gregor Damschen. 2015. 'Is the Idea of the Good Beyond Being? Plato's "Epekeina Tês Ousias" Revisited'. In *Second Sailing: Alternative Perspectives on Plato*, edited by Debra Nails and Harold Tarrant, 197–203. Espoo: Wellprint Oy.

Fraenkel, Carlos. 2015. 'Philosophy and Theology'. In *The Oxford Handbook of the Abrahamic Religions*, edited by Adam J. Silverstein, Guy G. Stroumsa, and Moshe Blidstein, 332–55. Oxford: Oxford University Press.

Frank, Richard M. 2005. 'The Neoplatonism of Jahm Ibn Ṣafwān'. In *Philosophy, Theology and Mysticism in Medieval Islam*, edited by Dimitri Gutas, 395–424. London: Routledge.

Franke, William. 2007. *On What Cannot Be Said: Apophatic Discourses in Philosophy, Religion, Literature, and the Arts, Vol. 1: Classic Formulations.* Notre Dame, IN: University of Notre Dame.

Gabirol, Ibn. 2005. *Fountain of Life (Fons Vitae).* Translated by Alfred B. Jacob. New York: Jewish Theological Seminary of America.

Gaiser, Konrad. 1980. 'Plato's Enigmatic Lecture "On the Good"'. *Phronesis* 25 (1): 5–37. https://doi.org/10.1163/156852880X00025.

Galluzzo, Gabriele, and Fabrizio Amerini, eds. 2013. *A Companion to the Latin Medieval Commentaries on Aristotle's Metaphysics.* Leiden: Brill.

Gericke, Jaco W. 2012. 'Philosophical Interpretations of Exodus 3: 14: A Brief Historical Overview'. *Journal for Semitics* 21 (1): 125–36.

Gersh, Stephen. 1986. *Middle Platonism and Neoplatonism: The Latin Tradition.* South Bend, IN: University of Notre Dame Press.

Gerson, Lloyd P. 2006. 'The "Holy Solemnity" of Forms and the Platonic Interpretation of Sophist'. *Ancient Philosophy* 26 (2): 291–304. https://doi.org/10.5840/ancientphil20062624.

2008. 'From Plato's Good to Platonic God'. *The International Journal of the Platonic Tradition* 2 (2): 93–112. https://doi.org/10.1163/187254708X 335746.

2020a. 'The Perennial Value of Platonism'. In *Christian Platonism: A History*, edited by Alexander J. B. Hampton and John Peter Kenney, 13–34. Cambridge: Cambridge University Press.

2020b. *Platonism and Naturalism: The Possibility of Philosophy*. Ithaca, NY: Cornell University Press.

Gersonides, Levi. 2008. 'Excerpts from the Wars of the Lord'. In *Medieval Jewish Philosophical Writings*, edited and translated by Charles Manekin, 153–91. Cambridge: Cambridge University Press. https://doi.org/10.1017/ CBO9780511811067.006.

Gilson, Étienne. 1952. *Being and Some Philosophers*. 2nd ed. Toronto: Pontifical Institute of Mediaeval Studies.

1994. *The Christian Philosophy of St. Thomas Aquinas*. Translated by Laurence Shook. Notre Dame, IN: University of Notre Dame Press.

2002. *Thomism: The Philosophy of Thomas Aquinas*. Translated by Armand Maurer and Laurence Shook. Toronto: Pontifical Institute of Mediaeval Studies.

Goodman, Lenn E., ed. 2012. *Neoplatonism and Jewish Thought*. Albany, NY: State University of New York Press.

Graham, Daniel W., ed. 2010. *The Texts of Early Greek Philosophy*. Vol. 1. Cambridge: Cambridge University Press.

Gregory of Nyssa. 2012. *Homilies on Ecclesiastes*. Translated by Stuart G. Hall and Rachel Moriarty. Berlin: De Gruyter.

2018. *Contra Eunomium I*. Edited by Miguel Brugarolas. Translated by Stuart George Hall. Leiden: Brill.

Greig, Jonathan. 2020. *The First Principle in Late Neoplatonism: A Study of the One's Causality in Proclus and Damascius*. Leiden: Brill.

Gschwandtner, Christina. 2013. *Postmodern Apologetics?: Arguments for God in Contemporary Philosophy*. New York: Fordham University Press.

Hadot, Pierre. 1963. 'La Distinction de l'être et de l'étant Dans Le De Hebdomadibus de Boèce'. In *Miscellanea Mediaevalia 2*, edited by Paul Wilpert, 147–53. Berlin: De Gruyter.

1968. *Porphyre et Victorinus*. Paris: Études augustiniennes.

Hägg, Henny Fiska. 2006. *Clement of Alexandria and the Beginnings of Christian Apophaticism*. Oxford: Oxford University Press.

Hampton, Alexander J. B., and John Peter Kenney. 2020. 'Christianity and Platonism'. In *Christian Platonism: A History*, edited by Alexander J. B. Hampton and John Peter Kenney, 3–9. Cambridge: Cambridge University Press.

Hankey, Wayne. 1980. 'Aquinas' First Principle: Being or Unity?' *Dionysius* 4: 133–72.

2004. 'Why Heidegger's "History" of Metaphysics Is Dead'. *American Catholic Philosophical Quarterly* 78 (3): 425–43.

Hart, David Bentley. 2008. 'The Hidden and the Manifest: Metaphysics after Nicaea'. In *Orthodox Readings of Augustine*, edited by George Demacopoulos and Aristotle Papanikolaou, 191–226. Crestwood, NY: St. Vladimir's Seminary Press.

Harvey, Steven. 2004. 'Islamic Philosophy and Jewish Philosophy'. In *The Cambridge Companion to Arabic Philosophy*, edited by Peter Adamson and Richard C. Taylor, 349–69. Cambridge: Cambridge University Press.

Heidegger, Martin. 1969. 'The Onto-Theo-Logical Constitution of Metaphysics'. In *Identity and Difference*, edited by Joan Stambaugh and translated by Joan Stambaugh, 42–74. New York: Harper & Row.

1998. 'Plato's Doctrine of Truth (1931/32, 1940)'. In *Pathmarks*, edited by William McNeill, translated by Thomas Sheehan, 155–82. Cambridge: Cambridge University Press.

2002. *On Time and Being*. Translated by Joan Stambaugh. Chicago, IL: University of Chicago Press.

Hildegard of Bingen. 1994. *The Letters of Hildegard of Bingen: Volume I*. Translated by Joseph L. Baird and Radd K. Ehrman. Oxford: Oxford University Press.

2018. *The Book of Divine Works*. Washington, DC: Catholic University of America Press.

Horan, Daniel P. 2014. *Postmodernity and Univocity: A Critical Account of Radical Orthodoxy and John Duns Scotus*. Minneapolis, MN: Fortress.

Iamblichus. 2003. *De mysteriis*. Translated by Emma C. Clarke, Jackson P. Hershbell, and John M. Dillon. Atlanta: Society of Biblical Literature.

Jacobs, Jonathan D. 2015. 'The Ineffable, Inconceivable, and Incomprehensible God: Fundamentality and Apophatic Theology'. *Oxford Studies in Philosophy of Religion* 6: 158–76. https://doi.org/10.1093/acprof:oso/9780198722335.003.0007.

Karamanolis, George E. 2006. *Plato and Aristotle in Agreement?: Platonists on Aristotle from Antiochus to Porphyry*. Oxford: Oxford University Press.

Kars, Aydogan. 2019. *Unsaying God: Negative Theology in Medieval Islam*. Oxford: Oxford University Press.

Kenney, John Peter. 2010. *Mystical Monotheism: A Study in Ancient Platonic Theology*. Eugene, OR: Wipf and Stock.

Khusrav, Nasir. 1949. *Six Chapters; or, Shish Fasl; Also Called Rawshana'i-Nama*. Translated by Wladimir Ivanow. Leiden: Brill.

Kooten, Geurt Hendrik van, ed. 2006. *The Revelation of the Name YHWH to Moses: Perspectives from Judaism, the Pagan Graeco-Roman World, and Early Christianity*. Leiden: Brill.

Krämer, Hans Joachim. 2012. 'Epekeina Tes Ousias: On Plato, Republic 509B'. In *The Other Plato: The Tübingen Interpretation of Plato's Inner-Academic Teachings*, edited by Dmitri Nikulin, 39–64. New York: SUNY Press.

Levinas, Emmanuel. 1991. *Otherwise than Being or Beyond Essence*. Translated by Alphonso Lingis. Dordrecht: Kluwer.

Lilla, Salvatore R. C. 1997. 'The Neoplatonic Hypostases and the Christian Trinity'. In *Studies in Plato and the Platonic Tradition*, edited by Mark Joyal, 127–89. London: Routledge.

Lizzini, Olga. 2003. 'Wuğūd-Mawğūd/Existence-Existent in Avicenna: A Key Ontological Notion of Arabic Philosophy'. *Quaestio* 3 (1): 111–38. https://doi.org/10.1484/j.quaestio.2.300319.

Lloyd, Antony C. 1970. 'The Later Neoplatonists'. In *The Cambridge History of Later Greek and Early Medieval Philosophy*, edited by Arthur H. Armstrong, 272–330. Cambridge: Cambridge University Press.

Lobel, Diana. 2020. 'Ehyeh Asher Ehyeh and the Tetragrammaton: Between Eternity and Necessary Existence in Saadya, Maimonides, and Abraham Maimonides'. *Review of Rabbinic Judaism* 23 (1): 89–126. https://doi.org/10.1163/15700704-12341365.

Lossky, Vladimir. 1957. *The Mystical Theology of the Eastern Church*. Cambridge: James Clarke.

Louth, Andrew. 1996. *Maximus the Confessor*. London: Routledge.

2001. *Denys the Areopagite*. London: Continuum.

2007. *The Origins of the Christian Mystical Tradition: From Plato to Denys*. 2nd ed. Oxford: Clarendon Press.

Marenbon, John. 2006. *Medieval Philosophy: An Historical and Philosophical Introduction*. New York: Routledge.

Marion, Jean-Luc. 1992. 'Is the Ontological Argument Ontological? The Argument According to Anselm and Its Metaphysical Interpretation According to Kant'. *Journal of the History of Philosophy* 30 (2): 201–18.

1995. *God Without Being: Hors-Texte*. Translated by Thomas A. Carlson. Chicago, IL: University of Chicago Press.

2003. 'Thomas Aquinas and Onto-Theo-Logy'. In *Mystics: Presence and Aporia*, edited by Christian Sheppard and Michael Kessler, 38–74. Chicago, IL: University of Chicago Press.

2005. 'God and the Gift: A Continental Perspective'. In *God's Advocates: Christian Thinkers in Conversation*, edited by Rupert Shortt. Grand Rapids: Eerdmans.

2012. *In the Self's Place: The Approach of Saint Augustine*. Translated by Jeffrey L. Kosky. Stanford: Stanford University Press.

Martyr, Justin. 2003. *Dialogue with Trypho*. Translated by Thomas B. Falls. Washington, DC: Catholic University of America Press.

McInerny, Ralph. 2012. *Boethius and Aquinas*. Washington, DC: Catholic University of America Press.

McIntosh, Mark A. 2021. *The Divine Ideas Tradition in Christian Mystical Theology*. Oxford: Oxford University Press.

Menn, Stephen. 1992. 'Aristotle and Plato on God as Nous and as the Good'. *The Review of Metaphysics* 45 (3): 543–73.

Meredith, Anthony. 2012. *Gregory of Nyssa*. London: Routledge.

Milbank, John. 2010. 'The Mystery of Reason'. In *The Grandeur of Reason: Religion, Tradition and Universalism*, edited by Peter Candler and Conor Cunningham, 68–117. London: SCM Press.

2018. 'The Dissolution of Divine Government: Gilson and the "Scotus Story"'. In *John Duns Scotus: Introduction to His Fundamental Positions*, edited by Etienne Gilson, translated by James Colbert, 538–76. London: T&T Clark.

Miner, Robert C. 2001. 'Suarez as Founder of Modernity: Reflections on a Topos in Recent Historiography'. *History of Philosophy Quarterly* 18 (1): 17–36.

Moore, Ian Alexander. 2018. 'The Problem of Ontotheology in Eckhart's Latin Writings'. *Epoché: A Journal for the History of Philosophy* 22 (2): 315–42. https://doi.org/10.5840/epoche201813105.

Moran, Dermot. 2004. *The Philosophy of John Scottus Eriugena: A Study of Idealism in the Middle Ages*. New York: Cambridge University Press.

Morewedge, Parviz, ed. 1992. *Neoplatonism and Islamic Thought*. Albany, NY: State University of New York Press.

Mortley, Raoul. 1986. *From Word to Silence II: The Way of Negation, Christian and Greek*. Bonn: Hanstein.

Noffke, Suzanne, trans. 1980. *Catherine of Siena: The Dialogue*. New York: Paulist Press.

O'Brien, Carl Séan. 2015. *The Demiurge in Ancient Thought: Secondary Gods and Divine Mediators*. Cambridge: Cambridge University Press.

Origen. 1953. *Contra Celsum*. Translated by Henry Chadwick. Cambridge: Cambridge University Press.

2006. *Commentary on the Gospel According to John, Books 13–32*. Translated by Ronald Heine. Washington, DC: Catholic University of America Press.

2017. *On First Principles*. Translated by John Behr. Oxford: Oxford University Press.

O'Rourke, Fran. 1992. *Pseudo-Dionysius and the Metaphysics of Aquinas*. Leiden: Brill.

Osborn, Eric. 1993. *The Emergence of Christian Theology*. Cambridge: Cambridge University Press.

Palamas, Gregory. 1983. *The Triads*. Translated by Nicholas Gendle. Mahwah, NJ: Paulist Press.

Palamas, Gregory. 1988. *The One Hundred and Fifty Chapters*. Translated by Robert E. Sinkewicz. Toronto: Pontifical Institute of Mediaeval Studies.

Pawl, Timothy. 2016. *In Defense of Conciliar Christology: A Philosophical Essay*. Oxford: Oxford University Press.

Peperzak, Adriaan T. 1998. 'Bonaventure's Contribution to the Twentieth Century Debate on Apophatic Theology'. *Faith and Philosophy* 15 (2): 181–92. https://doi.org/10.5840/faithphil199815215.

Perl, Eric D. 1991. *Methexis: Creation, Incarnation, Deification in Saint Maximus Confessor*. PhD Thesis. New Haven: Yale University.

1998. 'The Demiurge and the Forms: A Return to the Ancient Interpretation of Plato's Timaeus'. *Ancient Philosophy* 18 (1): 81–92. https://doi.org/10.5840/ancientphil19981816.

2007. *Theophany: The Neoplatonic Philosophy of Dionysius the Areopagite*. Albany, NY: State University of New York Press.

2011a. 'Esse Tantum and the One'. *Quaestiones Disputatae* 2 (1 & 2): 185–200.

2011b. 'Pseudo-Dionysius the Areopagite'. In *The Cambridge History of Philosophy in Late Antiquity*, vol. 2, edited by Lloyd P. Gerson, 767–87. Cambridge: Cambridge University Press.

2014. *Thinking Being: Introduction to Metaphysics in the Classical Tradition*. Leiden: Brill.

Pessin, Sarah. 2003. 'Jewish Neoplatonism: Being above Being and Divine Emanation in Solomon Ibn Gabirol and Isaac Israeli'. In *The Cambridge Companion to Medieval Jewish Philosophy*, edited by Daniel H. Frank and Oliver Leaman, 1st ed., 91–110. Cambridge: Cambridge University Press. https://doi.org/10.1017/CCOL0521652073.005.

Peterson, Sandra. 2019. 'Plato's Parmenides: A Reconsideration of Forms'. In *The Oxford Handbook of Plato*, edited by Gail Fine, 2nd ed., 231–60.

Oxford: Oxford University Press. https://doi.org/10.1093/oxfordhb/9780190639730.013.12.

Philo. 1929. *Philo: Volume II*. Translated by F. H. Colson and G. H. Whitaker. Loeb Classical Library. Cambridge, MA: Harvard University Press.

———. 1934. *Philo: Volume V*. Translated by F. H. Colson and G. H. Whitaker. Loeb Classical Library. Cambridge, MA: Harvard University Press.

———. 1935. *Philo: Volume VI*. Translated by F. H. Colson. Loeb Classical Library. Cambridge, MA: Harvard University Press.

Pickstock, Catherine. 2005. 'Duns Scotus: His Historical and Contemporary Significance'. *Modern Theology* 21 (4): 543–74. https://doi.org/10.1111/j.1468-0025.2005.00297.x.

Pines, Schlomo. 1971. 'Les Textes Arabes Dits Plotiniens et Le Courant "Porphyrien" Dans Le Néoplatonisme Grec'. In *Le Néoplatonisme*, edited by Pierre Hadot and Pierre-Maxime Schuhl, 303–13. Paris: CNRS.

Pino, Tikhon. 2022. *Essence and Energies: Being and Naming God in St Gregory Palamas*. New York: Routledge.

Plato. 1992. *Plato: Republic*. Translated by G. M. A. Grube and C. D. C. Reeve. Indianapolis, IN: Hackett.

———. 1996. *Parmenides*. Translated by Mary Louise Gill and Paul Ryan. Indianapolis, IN: Hackett.

———. 2008. *Timaeus and Critias*. Translated by Robin Waterfield. Oxford: Oxford University Press.

Plotinus. 2017. *The Enneads*. Translated by Lloyd P. Gerson. Cambridge: Cambridge University Press.

Pormann, Peter E., and Peter Adamson, trans. 2012. *The Philosophical Works of Al-Kindi*. Oxford: Oxford University Press.

Porphyry. 2005. *Sentences*. Edited by Luc Brisson. Translated by John Dillon. Paris: Vrin.

Proclus. 1963. *The Elements of Theology*. Translated by Eric R. Dodds. 2nd ed. Oxford: Oxford University Press.

———. 1992. *Commentary on Plato's Parmenides*. Translated by Glenn Raymond Morrow and John M. Dillon. Princeton, NJ: Princeton University Press.

———. 2008. *Commentary on Plato's Timaeus*. Translated by David Runia and Michael Share. Vol. 2. Cambridge: Cambridge University Press.

———. 2014. *On the Existence of Evils*. Translated by Carlos Steel and Jan Opsomer. London: Bloomsbury.

———. 2018. *Commentary on Plato's Republic*. Translated by Dirk Baltzly, John Finamore, and Graeme Miles. Vol. 2. Cambridge: Cambridge University Press.

Pseudo-Dionysius. 1987. *Pseudo-Dionysius: The Complete Works*. Translated by Colm Luibheid. New York: Paulist Press.

Quḍāt, ʿAyn al-. 2022. *The Essence of Reality: A Defense of Philosophical Sufism*. Translated by Mohammed Rustom, 27. New York: New York University Press.

Radde-Gallwitz, Andrew. 2020. 'The One and the Trinity'. In *Christian Platonism: A History*, edited by Alexander J. B. Hampton and John Peter Kenney, 53–78. Cambridge: Cambridge University Press.

Rea, Michael C. 2018. *The Hiddenness of God*. Oxford: Oxford University Press.

——— 2020. 'God beyond Being: Towards a Credible Account of Divine Transcendence'. In *Essays in Analytic Theology: Volume 1*, edited by Michael C. Rea, 120–38. Oxford: Oxford University Press. https://doi .org/10.1093/oso/9780198866800.003.0007.

Rettig, John W., trans. 1988. *St. Augustine: Tractates on the Gospel of John 1– 10*. Washington, DC: Catholic University of America Press.

Reydams-Schils, Gretchen. 2020. *Calcidius on Plato's Timaeus: Greek Philosophy, Latin Reception, and Christian Contexts*. Cambridge: Cambridge University Press.

Richard of Saint Victor. 2011. *On the Trinity*. Translated by Ruben Angelici. Eugene, OR: Wipf and Stock.

Riel, Gerd Van. 2016. 'The One, the Henads, and the Principles'. In *All From One: A Guide to Proclus*, edited by Pieter d'Hoine and Marije Martijn, 73–97. New York: Oxford University Press.

Rist, John M. 1962. 'Theos and the One in Some Texts of Plotinus'. *Mediaeval Studies* 24 (January): 169–80. https://doi.org/10.1484/J.MS.2.306785.

——— 1967. *Plotinus: Road to Reality*. Cambridge: Cambridge University Press.

——— 2007. 'Augustine, Aristotelianism, and Aquinas: Three Varieties of Philosophical Adaptation'. In *Aquinas the Augustinian*, edited by Michael Dauphinais, Barry David, and Matthew Levering, 79–99. Washington, DC: Catholic University of America Press.

Rocca, Gregory. 2004. *Speaking the Incomprehensible God: Thomas Aquinas on the Interplay of Positive and Negative Theology*. Washington, DC: Catholic University of America Press.

Rosheger, John P. 2001. 'Boethius and the Paradoxical Mode of Theological Discourse'. *American Catholic Philosophical Quarterly* 75 (3): 323–43. https://doi.org/10.5840/acpq200175318.

——— 2002. 'Is God a "What?": Avicenna, William of Auvergne, and Aquinas on the Divine Essence'. In *Medieval Philosophy and the Classical Tradition*, edited by John Inglis, 233–49. London: Routledge.

Rubenstein, Mary-Jane. 2003. 'Unknow Thyself: Apophaticism, Deconstruction, and Theology after Ontotheology'. *Modern Theology* 19 (3): 387–417. https://doi.org/10.1111/1468-0025.00228.

Safi, Omid. 2006. *The Politics of Knowledge in Premodern Islam: Negotiating Ideology and Religious Inquiry*. Chapel Hill: University of North Carolina Press.

Schaff, Philip, ed. 1885. *Clement of Alexandria*. Translated by William Wilson. Grand Rapids, MI: Christian Classics Ethereal Library.

Scholem, Gershom. 1974. *Kabbalah*. New York: Meridian.

Segal, Aaron. 2021. 'His Existence Is Essentiality: Maimonides as Metaphysician'. In *Maimonides' Guide of the Perplexed: A Critical Guide*, edited by Daniel Frank and Aaron Segal, 102–24. Cambridge: Cambridge University Press.

Shaw, Gregory. 1995. *Theurgy and the Soul: The Neoplatonism of Iamblichus*. University Park: Pennsylvania State University Press.

Sheldon-Williams, I. P., ed. 1968. *Johannis Scotti Eriugenae: Periphyseon (De Diuisione Naturae)*. Translated by I. P. Sheldon-Williams. 4 vols. Dublin: The Dublin Institute for Advanced Studies.

Shem Tov b. Joseph Falaquera and Solomon ibn Gabirol. 2008. 'Excerpts from "The Source of Life"'. In *Medieval Jewish Philosophical Writings*, edited and translated by Charles Manekin, 23–87. Cambridge: Cambridge University Press. https://doi.org/10.1017/CBO9780511811067.006.

Simplicius. 2012. *On Aristotle Physics 1.5–9*. Translated by Han Baltussen, Michael Atkinson, Ian Mueller, and Michael Share. London: Bloomsbury.

Sparrow, Tom. 2014. *The End of Phenomenology: Metaphysics and the New Realism*. Edinburgh: Edinburgh University Press.

Sterling, Gregory E. 2014. 'The People of the Covenant or the People of God: Exodus in Philo of Alexandria'. In *The Book of Exodus: Composition, Reception, and Interpretation*, edited by Thomas B. Dozeman, Craig A. Evans, and Joel N. Lohr, 404–39. Leiden: Brill.

Stump, Eleonore. 2018. 'The Personal God of Classical Theism'. In *The Question of God's Perfection*, edited by Yoram Hazony and Dru Johnson, 65–81. Leiden: Brill.

Sweeney, Leo. 1992. *Divine Infinity in Greek and Medieval Thought*. New York: P. Lang.

Tarán, Leonardo. 2016. *Speusippus of Athens: A Critical Study with a Collection of the Related Texts and Commentary*. Leiden: Brill.

Taylor, Richard C. 1998. 'Aquinas, the "Plotiniana Arabica," and the Metaphysics of Being and Actuality'. *Journal of the History of Ideas* 59 (2): 217–39. https://doi.org/10.2307/3653974.

2012. 'Primary Causality and Ibda' (Creare) in the Liber de Causis'. In *Wahrheit Und Geschichte: Die Gebrochene Tradition Metaphysischen Denkens*, edited by Günther Mensching and Alia Mensching-Estakhr, 115–36. Würzburg: Königshausen & Neumann.

2020. 'Contextualizing the Kalām Fī Maḥḍ Al-Khair / Liber de Causis'. In *Reading Proclus and the Book of Causes, Volume 2: Translations and Acculturations*, edited by Dragos Calma, 211–32. Leiden: Brill.

Thillet, Pierre. 1971. 'Indices Porphyriens Dans La Théologie d'Aristote'. In *Le Néoplatonisme*, edited by Pierre Hadot and Pierre-Maxime Schuhl, 292–302. Paris: CNRS.

Tobon, Monica. 2022. 'Bonaventure and Dionysius'. In *The Oxford Handbook of Dionysius the Areopagite*, edited by Dimitrios Pallis, Mark Edwards, and Georgios Steiris, 350–66. Oxford: Oxford University Press.

Tomassi, Chiara O. 2022. 'Once Again: Marius Victorinus and Gnosticism'. In *The Philosophy, Theology, and Rhetoric of Marius Victorinus*, edited by Stephen A. Cooper and Václav Němec, 457–80. Atlanta: SBL Press.

Turner, Denys. 2004. *Faith, Reason and the Existence of God*. Cambridge: Cambridge University Press.

Turner, John. 2001. *Sethian Gnosticism and the Platonic Tradition*. Quebec: Presses Université Laval.

2007. 'Victorinus, Parmenides Commentaries and the Platonizing Sethian Treatises'. In *Platonisms: Ancient, Modern, and Postmodern*, edited by Kevin Corrigan and John Turner, 53–96. Leiden: Brill.

Turner, John, and Kevin Corrigan, eds. 2011a. *Plato's Parmenides and Its Heritage Vol. 1, History and Interpretation from the Old Academy to Later Platonism and Gnosticism*. Leiden: Brill.

eds. 2011b. *Plato's Parmenides and Its Heritage Vol. 2, Its Reception in Neoplatonic, Jewish, and Christian Texts*. Leiden: Brill.

Twetten, David. 2015. 'Aristotelian Cosmology and Causality in Classical Arabic Philosophy and Its Greek Background'. In *Ideas in Motion in Baghdad and Beyond*, edited by Damien Janos, 312–434. Leiden: Brill.

Undusk, Rein. 2009. 'Infinity on the Threshold of Christianity: The Emergence of a Positive Concept Out of Negativity'. *Trames* 13 (4): 307–40.

2012. 'Faith and Reason: Charting the Medieval Concept of the Infinite'. *Trames* 16 (1): 4–45.

Vargas, Rosa E. 2013. 'Albert on Being and Beings: The Doctrine of Esse'. In *A Companion to Albert the Great: Theology, Philosophy, and the Sciences*, edited by Irven Resnick, 627–47. Leiden: Brill.

Velde, Rudi A. te. 1995. *Participation and Substantiality in Thomas Aquinas*. Leiden: Brill.

2020. 'Participation: Aquinas and His Neoplatonic Sources'. In *Christian Platonism: A History*, edited by Alexander J. B. Hampton and John Peter Kenney, 122–39. Cambridge: Cambridge University Press.

Victorinus, Marius. 1981. *Theological Treatises on the Trinity*. Translated by Mary T. Clark. Washington, DC: Catholic University of America Press.

Walzer, Richard, trans. 1985. *Al-Farabi on The Perfect State: Abū Naṣr Al-Fārābī's Mabādi' Ārā' Ahl Al-Madīna Al-Fāḍila*. Oxford: Oxford University Press.

Watson, Nicholas, and Jacqueline Jenkins, eds. 2006. *The Writings of Julian of Norwich*. University Park, PA: Pennsylvania State University Press.

Wear, Sarah Klitenic. 2011. 'Activity and Potentiality in Augustine and Victorinus' Use of Jn 5:19'. *Quaestiones Disputatae* 2 (1): 107–17. https://doi.org/10/f2tswq.

Weedman, Mark. 2010. 'The Polemical Context of Gregory of Nyssa's Doctrine of Divine Infinity'. *Journal of Early Christian Studies* 18 (1): 81–104. https://doi.org/10.1353/earl.0.0301.

Whittaker, John. 1967. 'Moses Atticizing'. *Phoenix* 21 (3): 196–201. https://doi.org/10/bp5j6 t.

1969. 'Epekeina Nou Kai Ousias'. *Vigiliae Christianae* 23 (2): 91–104. https://doi.org/10/cgfj56.

Widdicombe, Peter. 1994. *The Fatherhood of God from Origen to Athanasius*. Oxford: Oxford University Press.

Wilkinson, Robert. 2015. *Tetragrammaton: Western Christians and the Hebrew Name of God: From the Beginnings to the Seventeenth Century*. Leiden: Brill.

Williams, Rowan. 2002. *Arius: Heresy and Tradition*. Grand Rapids: Eerdmans.

Wippel, John F. 2000. *The Metaphysical Thought of Thomas Aquinas: From Finite Being to Uncreated Being*. Washington, DC: Catholic University of America Press.

Wisse, Frederik, and Michael Waldstein, eds. 1995. *The Apocryphon of John*. Leiden: Brill.

Yannaras, Christos. 2005. *On the Absence and Unknowability of God: Heidegger and the Areopagite*. Translated by Haralambos Ventis. London: T&T Clark.

2007. *Person and Eros*. Translated by Norman Russell. Brookline, MA: Holy Cross Orthodox Press.

Acknowledgements

I am indebted to many colleagues and friends for conversations and advice in writing this study. For assistance great and small, I thank Angus Brook, David Bronstein, Renee Köhler-Ryan, Joseph Wood, Andrew Davison, Gaven Kerr, and Lloyd Gerson. For assistance on Greek and Coptic language matters, I thank Lucy Smith and Sam Kaldas. I am grateful to series editors Chad Meister and Paul Moser for their guidance and patience, and I am obliged to two anonymous reviewers of the manuscript, whose critical comments prompted some important revisions and additions. I thank Chris Wilcox for her generous Blue Mountains hospitality while I worked on Section 2. I am most grateful to my wife, Kate, and our little ones, Halle and Hugh, who were each accommodating in their own ways as I worked on this manuscript. The Good is the light of being, Plato says – these three are the lights of my life.

For Hugh. Birth is the gift of being, and what a gift yours was.

Cambridge Elements ☰

Religion and Monotheism

Paul K. Moser

Loyola University Chicago

Paul K. Moser is Professor of Philosophy at Loyola University Chicago. He is the author of *Paul's Gospel of Divine Self-Sacrifice; The Divine Goodness of Jesus; Divine Guidance; Understanding Religious Experience; The God Relationship; The Elusive God* (winner of national book award from the Jesuit Honor Society); *The Evidence for God; The Severity of God; Knowledge and Evidence* (all Cambridge University Press); and *Philosophy after Objectivity* (Oxford University Press); co-author of *Theory of Knowledge* (Oxford University Press); editor of *Jesus and Philosophy* (Cambridge University Press) and *The Oxford Handbook of Epistemology* (Oxford University Press); co-editor of *The Wisdom of the Christian Faith* (Cambridge University Press). He is the co-editor with Chad Meister of the book series *Cambridge Studies in Religion, Philosophy, and Society.*

Chad Meister

Affiliate Scholar, Ansari Institute for Global Engagement with Religion, University of Notre Dame

Chad Meister is Affiliate Scholar at the Ansari Institute for Global Engagement with Religion at the University of Notre Dame. His authored and co-authored books include *Evil: A Guide for the Perplexed* (Bloomsbury Academic, 2nd edition); *Introducing Philosophy of Religion* (Routledge); *Introducing Christian Thought* (Routledge, 2nd edition); and *Contemporary Philosophical Theology* (Routledge). He has edited or co-edited the following: *The Oxford Handbook of Religious Diversity* (Oxford University Press); *Debating Christian Theism* (Oxford University Press); with Paul Moser, *The Cambridge Companion to the Problem of Evil* (Cambridge University Press); and with Charles Taliaferro, *The History of Evil* (Routledge, in six volumes). He is the co-editor with Paul Moser of the book series *Cambridge Studies in Religion, Philosophy, and Society.*

About the Series

This Cambridge Element series publishes original concise volumes on monotheism and its significance. Monotheism has occupied inquirers since the time of the Biblical patriarch, and it continues to attract interdisciplinary academic work today. Engaging, current, and concise, the Elements benefit teachers, researched, and advanced students in religious studies, Biblical studies, theology, philosophy of religion, and related fields.

Cambridge Elements ☰

Religion and Monotheism

Elements in the Series

A full series listing is available at: www.cambridge.org/er&m

Printed in the USA
CPSIA information can be obtained
at www.ICGtesting.com
CBHW071929030924
13955CB00010B/1008

9 781009 012768